NOT YOUR MOTHER'S COOKBOOK

UNUSUAL RECIPES
FOR THE ADVENTUROUS COOK

Crown Roast of Hot Dog,
one of 174 recipes in this book that are interesting, unusual, achievable, tasty,
and unlikely to be served by your mother.

NOT YOUR MOTHER'S COOKBOOK

UNUSUAL RECIPES
FOR THE ADVENTUROUS COOK

MARINA AND JOHN BEAR
INTRODUCTION BY JAY CONRAD LEVINSON
FOREWORD BY MARGARET FOX

SLG Books
Berkeley/Hong Kong

NOT YOUR MOTHER'S COOKBOOK

SLG BOOKS
PO Box 9465 Berkeley, CA 94709
Tel. (510) 525-1134
Fax: (510) 525-2632
Email NotYourMother@slgbooks.com
URL: www.slgbooks.com

Library of Congress Cataloging-in-Publication Data

Bear, Marina, 1941-
  Not your mother's cookbook : unusual recipes for the adventurous cook
/ Marina and John Bear ; introduction by Jay Conrad Levinson ; foreword
by Margaret Fox.
      p. cm.
  ISBN 0-943389-37-2
  1. Cookery. I. Bear, John, 1938- II. Title.
TX714 .B3853 2002
641.5—dc21

                        2002030872

Printed in Hong Kong

TABLE OF CONTENTS

INTRODUCTIONS

APPETIZERS

SOUPS

MAIN DISHES

VEGETABLES AND SALADS

BREADS

SANDWICHES

EGGS AND BREAKFAST ITEMS

DESSERTS AND CANDY

GUERILLA COOKING

An introduction by
Jay Conrad Levinson
Author of *Guerilla Marketing*

I certainly do not advise you to take a cookbook into the bathroom, but I have to let you know that "Not Your Mother's Cookbook" makes for such superb reading that you will want to enjoy it for a lot more than recipes.

The recipes, incidentally, are also good. They are for the adventurous cook and the cook's adventurous guests. Don't let the names of the dishes — such as 'Pinto Bean Fudge' — throw you into a fit of laughter before you taste them. Truly, they are as delicious as they are unique.

If you've always dreamt of your guests commenting upon the meal you served to them, there is no question that these dishes will make your dream come true.

And you won't have to scout out hard-to-find grocery stores to find your ingredients. Almost any supermarket will have exactly what you need.

This may not be your mother's cookbook, but dear old mom would be very proud of you if she tasted your brave cuisine. She'll have as much fun dining upon it as you will in cooking it. Rarely is an appetizer the topic of after-dinner conversation, but any appetizer (or soup or dessert or bread) from this cookbook will enliven the talk after the diners complete their meal.

You, just like me, probably have a whole shelf of wonderful cookbooks. But none of them are even remotely close to this one. And none supply the recipes for dishes even vaguely reminiscent of the meals contained in these pages. They are so scrumptious and nourishing that you shouldn't be surprised if a chain of 'Not Your Mother's Restaurants" springs up coast-to-coast, not to mention France and Japan. Be warned, Colonel Sanders.

I know that many cooks, both professional and otherwise, scour the world for unique recipes and meals. The good news is that they can limit their scouring to these pages, knowing they'll discover dishes that they'd never find elsewhere. The bad news is that this wondrous book will most likely never be made into a movie.

As the author of umpteen books called "Guerrilla Marketing" or "Guerrilla Advertising" or "Guerrilla Creativity," I'm surprised that Marina and John Bear didn't name this one "Guerrilla Cooking." Then again, your mother may have tried a few guerrilla recipes, but you can be sure that she never prepared a meal like those in these pages. These may be meals that she'd love and cherish, but there's no question that this is not her cookbook.

If you're smart, you'll make it your cookbook. And you'll become famous for your cooking as a result. Should you be a meat-and-potatoes kind of person, this book will change your life — and it's not even a self-help book.

But it is a riotous and valuable cookbook. And I hope like crazy that you'll invite me for dinner after you've read it.

Jay Conrad Levinson
Author, the *Guerrilla Marketing* series of books
Marin County, California
Fall, 2002

Jay Conrad Levinson has neither required nor even asked that we say this, but we are grateful for his kind words, and would like to repay him, as it were, by inviting you to read his splendid books on guerilla marketing and other related topics. You'll find them in any bookstore, and online at www.jayconradlevinson.com. And the same goes . . .

FOREWORD

Margaret Fox

For many years, owner-chef of Cafe Beaujolais, Mendocino, California
Co-Author of *Cafe Beaujolais, Morning Food,* and *Evening Food*

You have eaten a lot of food in your life. You probably think you know a fair amount about it. Well, forget it. This book dispels the notion that there is nothing new under the sun.

John and Marina Bear, two of the wackiest brilliant people I know, have assembled a group of recipes, the likes of which you have never seen—combinations so strange you will wonder if there's been a misprint. But no, I assure you they are not just a mess of ingredients thrown together for the sake of being creative. These recipes taste good too.

Go ahead, be suspicious as you enter the kitchen, but after your successes start to roll out of there, concern will be replaced by confidence. You'll never look hopelessly in the cupboard and fridge again and wail, "I can't make anything out of this stuff." Check what these guys have to offer first.

. . . for Margaret Fox, friend and co-author of three *Cafe Beaujolais* cookbooks during the ten years we lived in Mendocino. Now she has sold Cafe Beaujolais, and is in the business of business consulting and coaching for the bewildered professional. This practical and talented woman can be found at (707) 937-0618, mfox@mcn.org. And the first she'll know of this shameless plug is when she reads it in the finished book.

A FEW WORDS (497, TO BE PRECISE) FROM THE AUTHORS

Hello. Let's say you've called us up on your cell phone at this very instant and said, "Hey, Marina and John, I'm standing here in the bookstore trying to decide whether to buy your book for myself, or as a gift, and I wonder if you can tell me why I should choose yours, instead of one of the other 42,000 on the shelves. Oh, and please limit your response to two words or less." Here's what we'd say:

"They work."

The recipes work. They are do-able, and you'll be glad when you are done. There are lots of cookbooks out there that are fun to read, but the recipes are either so complicated or require such exotic ingredients (such as rare spices) or unappetizing ingredients (such as raccoons), that you'd probably never try one. And, sadly, there are more than a few books out there whose recipes went right from some other book into print, without passing through a kitchen to be tested.

We set about to assemble (and create) a whole bunch of recipes that had these three characteristics:

• They are truly unusual (unusual food combinations, unusual preparation methods, unusual stories)

• They work. You can really make them, and you (and your table companions) will be glad that you did. (Note: see the *Extreme Cuisine* box below!)

To this end, we made use of a veritable platoon of volunteer testers, headed by our own twin daughters, one a professionally trained chef, the other a darned good cook, and both ruthless in their evaluations. You'll never see the more-than-100 recipes that were tossed out. We offer you the winners. We hope you have as much fun with them as we did, and when you come upon one that just boggles the mind and maybe the taste buds too, well, just recall one of the oldest relevant proverbs on the books: *De gustibus non disputandum*—there's just no accounting for tastes.

One of the authors of this book is an ethicist and insisted on creating this section. When we'd chosen the 160-or-so recipes for this book, there were, left over, roughly a dozen more that looked really interesting, but, for one reason (took months to prepare) or another (forgot), we simply did not get around to testing properly. We could have left them out; we could have sneaked them in. But we chose the middle ground of including them, but with an alert: *Extreme Cuisine.* Try these at your own risk. If any of your results are moldy, unusually smelly, or seem to be inhabited, don't even try them. You have just created a conversation piece, not a meal. Encase whatever it was in plastic and use it for a paperweight, doorstop, or garden ornament. So when you see that symbol on the left at the top of a recipe, you'll know. If you choose to share your results and opinions with us, we'll be glad to hear from you, in care of the publisher. Thank you.

APPLE, SARDINE, AND CHOPPED LIVER APPETIZERS

A s far as we know (and we have checked our 4-volume *History of the Sardine,* and perused the www.sardine.com site), no one in the history of food-assembling has ever thought of combining the above three ingredients until we did so, and more's the pity. They go together extremely well.

Ingredients
1   apple
    chopped liver
    sardines
    crackers, melba toast, or bread

Preparation
• Smear the chopped liver on the crackers or whatever (We prefer melba toast.).
• Peel the apple, core it, and cut it into quarters.
• Now cut each quarter into quarters.
• Place 2 or 3 apple pieces into the liver on each cracker.
• Top with one big sardine.

Note: if the sardines are oily, blot them gently with paper towels first. If someone comes into the kitchen at this point and says, "What *are* you doing?" you can smile sweetly and reply, "Oh, I'm just blotting my sardines. Do you have any problem with that?"

BLEU CHEESECAKE

We all know about the dessert called cheesecake, commonly made with cream cheese. Now Peggy Battles, in Amarillo, Texas, has shared with us her recipe for the *appetizer* called "cheesecake," but in this instance, it is made with that lovely moldy almost-sour stuff called blue or bleu (or, presumably, *azul* or *blau*, etc., depending on where you are) cheese. In any event, it makes a fine and unexpected appetizer.

Ingredients
1   cup crushed cheese crackers
2   tbsp. butter
1   pound cream cheese, softened
8   ounces blue cheese
3   eggs
¼   cup flour
¼   tsp. salt
¼   cup picante sauce
1   cup sour cream
½   cup chopped green onions
½   cup chopped walnuts

Preparation
• Preheat oven to 325°.
• Butter a 10-inch springform pan.
• Sprinkle cracker crumbs on the bottom and sides.
• Mix cheeses, eggs, flour, salt, picante sauce, and sour cream.
• Fold in the onions. Pour the mixture into the pan, and sprinkle with walnuts.
• Bake for 1 hour.
• Cool and chill overnight.
• Serve at room temperature, with extra crackers, if desired.

Serves 10

BOURBON AND SHERRIED CHICKEN LIVER PATÉ
WITH WALNUTS

This is an ordinary, typical chicken liver paté. Except that it is made with sherry. And a healthy dollop of bourbon. And nutmeg. Oh, and lots of toasted walnuts. Say, maybe it isn't so ordinary after all. Warning: the bourbon isn't cooked, so it remains just as potent as when it left the distillery, which you might bear in mind before offering second helpings to the ladies from the Temperance Union.

Ingredients

¾ cup corn oil
1 small onion
1 pound chicken livers
1½ cups chicken broth
2 tbsp. sherry
¾ tsp. paprika
⅛ tsp. nutmeg

½ tsp. salt
⅛ tsp. pepper
1 clove garlic
½ cup bourbon
1 envelope unflavored gelatin
1 cup toasted chopped walnuts

Preparation

• Heat the oil in a large frying pan.
• Chop the onion and add it, along with the livers, to the heated oil.
• Cook for 10 minutes, stirring 2 or 3 times.
• Add the sherry, paprika, salt, pepper, minced garlic, and nutmeg.
• Cook for 5 minutes over medium heat, uncovered. Stir occasionally.
• Remove from the stove and add the bourbon.
• Pour ¾ cup unheated chicken broth into a blender or food processor. Sprinkle on the gelatin and let it stand for 3 minutes to soften. Heat the remaining broth and pour over the gelatin. Blend, or process, until the gelatin has dissolved.
• Add ½ of the chicken liver mixture to the gelatin and broth and blend until smooth. Repeat with the remaining liver.
• Decant into a serving bow, stir in the walnuts, and chill until firm.

Serves 6 to 8

DO IT YOURSELF HAWAIIAN JERKY

It sounds like a child's riddle: How do you make a Hawaiian jerky? (Put itching powder in her grass skirt?) But it is actually an uncommon and delicious snack, easily made by anyone who lives in a place likely to have three days of sunshine in a row.

Hawaiian jerky, in case such things interest you, is different from (and, we think, much tastier than) ordinary convenience store jerky, because it is marinated in soy sauce and ginger instead of plain old brine.

Ingredients
4   pounds beef (or venison)
3   tsp. freshly-grated ginger
2   cups soy sauce
2   cloves garlic, minced
⅓   cup coarse salt
1   tsp. pepper (coarse-ground)
1   tbsp. sugar

Preparation
• Trim all the fat from the meat and cut it into strips ¼-inch thick and about 2 inches wide by 4 inches long. (The length and width may vary.)
• Lay the strips out in a large glass bowl or baking dish.
• Mix together the soy sauce, salt, sugar, ginger, and minced garlic, and pepper.
• Pour this marinade over the meat.
• Refrigerate, covered, for at least 24 hours, turning it two or three times.
• Now the meat is ready for drying (or jerking). It should hang in the warm sunshine for three full days. You can pin it to a clothesline, nail it to a fence post, or, if you are infested with insects, you may have to rig up some sort of a screened box. In dry climates, you can leave it out all night; otherwise, bring it inside at sunset, or on damp or cloudy days. Jerky will keep for at least a year without refrigeration.

How many it serves depends on how well you like it. This recipe makes anywhere from a two week to a 34-year supply.

FLAMING HERRING

Some dishes are served flaming solely for the spectacular effect. Some are flamed because it actually enhances the flavor of the food being set ablaze. And some are simply to satisfy the pyromaniacal tendencies of the chef. Flaming herring actually has some elements of all three. A herring on fire may not be beautiful, but it certainly is interesting. It undeniably improves the taste. And until you've done it, you just can't imagine what a thrill it is to set the torch to a kipper.

Ingredients

6   smoked herrings
3   tbsp. butter
1   tbsp. lemon juice
⅓   cup bourbon (Scotch will do)
     pepper

Preparation

• Sauté the herrings in a saucepan or chafing dish, in the butter and lemon juice until hot.
• Add pepper (preferably fresh-ground).
• Warm the bourbon in a saucepan, ignite, and pour over the herring.
• Serve while flaming on preheated plates.

Serves 3 or 4

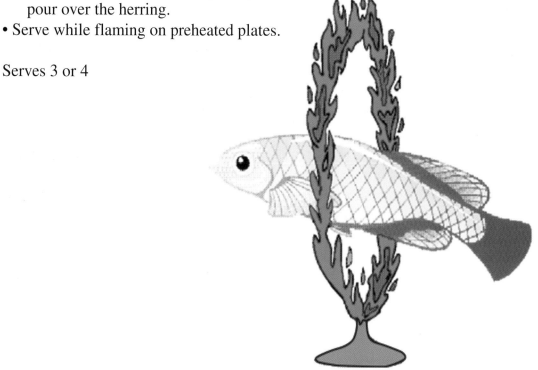

HOT MARSHMALLOW AND FRANKFURTER HORS D'OEUVRES

The two go together very nicely, especially when combined with sweet potatoes on a little biscuit. If you can coerce people into taking the first bite, your only problem thereafter will be manufacturing enough of them to keep people happy. This is especially good to make when you're having adults and children over. The kids love them, the parents indulgently taste them, and then you discover that you have to go and make another batch because everybody has polished them off.

Ingredients

biscuit dough for 8 biscuits (Yes, you can use the biscuit-dough-in-a-tube that's usually found near the eggs in your supermarket.)
3   cooked frankfurters
8   marshmallows
1   sweet potato

Preparation

• Cook and mash the sweet potato.
• Roll out the biscuit dough about ¼ inch thick, and cut it into circles 4 inches in diameter.
• Put the dough into small muffin tins, custard cups, or brioche tins.
• Put a heaping teaspoon of sweet potato on the bottom.
• Arrange on this four thin frankfurter slices.
• On top of this, arrange four thin marshmallow slices. (Cut each marshmallow into four horizontal slices using a pair of wet scissors.)
• Bake in a 400° oven until the biscuits start turning golden brown (about 10 to 12 minutes).

Serves 8

SALMON JALAPEÑO HORS D'OEUVRES

When our request for unusual recipes went out over the internet, one of the first replies was from Christine Smith, somewhere out there in cyberspace, who was kind enough to share her recipe for this spicy hors d'oeuvre—sufficiently spicy that she recommends wearing plastic gloves during the preparation. No, not for opening the cans of salmon, silly.

Ingredients

20   fresh jalepeños
8   ounces sour cream
8   ounces cream cheese, at room temperature
2   small (tuna size) cans of salmon
    onion and garlic powder to taste
    a few drops of liquid smoke
    salt and pepper to taste

Preparation

• Wearing plastic gloves, wash and split the jalepeños lengthwise leaving on the stem (which will serve as a little handle later).
• Clean out all the seeds and the white fibers inside and soak in cold water.
• Open salmon cans and drain all the juice.
• In a mixing bowl, combine the cream cheese and sour cream. Add the salmon, and liquid smoke.
• Season with the onion and garlic powder.
• Take the jalepeños out of the water and towel dry.
• Stuff each half with the salmon mixture.
• Arrange them in a single layer on a tray and refrigerate until ready to serve.

Makes 40 hors d'oeuvres

SHRIMP CHRISTMAS TREE A LA UNCLE SAM

Do you know what the Bureau of Commercial Fisheries of the United States Department of Agriculture does? Neither did we, until we came upon their utterly splendid plans for a display to celebrate the birth of Jesus Christ by impaling three pounds of shrimp onto a styrofoam cone and calling it a Christmas Tree. As Uncle Sam says, "Leafy green endive duplicates crisp holly, while ever-popular shrimp add shape and color interest to this creative conversation piece."

We trust that the Bureau is now hard at work on plans for making other religious symbols out of seafood of other shapes and sizes.

Ingredients

3   pounds cooked shrimp
2   quarts water
½   cup salt
     cocktail sauce
1   styrofoam cone, 2½ feet high
1   styrofoam square, 1 foot square
4   large bunches curly endive
     toothpicks

Preparation

• Trace the base of the cone onto the square, and a cut circular piece out of the square base for the cone to stand in.
• Cover the base and the entire cone with overlapping leaves of endive, applied with half toothpicks.
• Attach shrimps to the tree with toothpicks.
• Merry Christmas.

Note: styrofoam cones and squares can be bought at craft shops or in the craft departments of superstores that have "Mart" in their names.

TEXAS CAVIAR AND NEW JERSEY CAVIAR

With a pound of authentic sturgeon-egg caviar selling for the equivalent of a week's wages, non-wealthy people in various parts of the world have come up with interesting substitutions: something tasty and semi-elegant to spread on thin toast or crackers for an appetizer. Here are two versions we like: Texas Caviar, as served in Amarillo by Peggy Battles, and the version Marina grew up with in New Jersey, where her Russian immigrant forbears called it Baklavana Ikra, or eggplant caviar.

TEXAS CAVIAR

Ingredients

2	20-ounce cans black-eyed peas, drained		¼	cup jalapeño pepper, seeded and chopped
1	large jar Picante sauce (medium or hot)		1	cup green onions and tops, chopped
1	16-ounce can white hominy (drained)		1	tbsp. sugar
1	cup red bell pepper, chopped		1	tbsp. salt
1	cup onion, chopped		2	tbsp. black pepper
1	cup fresh tomatoes, chopped		2	tbsp. cumin
½	cup fresh cilantro, chopped			

Preparation

Mix. Refrigerate. Serve.

NEW JERSEY CAVIAR

Ingredients

1	large eggplant, peeled and sliced into 1/2 inch thick slices		1	large green pepper
¼	cup olive oil		4	cloves of garlic, pressed
2	onions		1	small can tomato paste
4	ribs of celery		1	lemon

Preparation

• Steam the eggplant until it is thoroughly soft. Cool.
• In a food processor, mince fine the onions, celery, and green pepper.
• Heat 2 tbsp. oil in a large skillet or saute pan. Add onions, celery, and pepper.
• Cook over medium heat, stirring, for 10 minutes. Add the garlic and continue

to cook for 5 minutes, stirring.

- Whirl the eggplant in the food processor for a few seconds to chop it and add it to the pan along with the tomato paste.
- At this point, you can do one of two things: Either lower the heat under the pan as low as it will go, cover, and cook for an hour, stirring occasionally. Or you can turn the caviar into a large baking dish, cover it, and bake it for 1½ hours at 250°.
- When it is thoroughly cooked, so there is no crunch of celery or onion, remove from the heat and allow to cool.
- Add the juice of the lemon and 2 tbsp. oil.
- Season with salt and pepper to taste. Chill.
- Serve with lavash or sesame crackers or just eat it with a spoon straight out of the dish in the refrigerator.

SOUPS

ZEN SOUP
(made with clear broth,
one noodle, and one kernel of corn)

BORSCHT WITH CHERRIES AND HONEY
(OR CHERRY SOUP WITH HONEY AND BORSCHT)

The principle reason that fruity soups are rarely seen as a soup course is that they are often pretty dreadful. There are, happily, some exceptions. One of the strangest (and best) of these is this curious item, which should be served very cold on a very hot July night. Or, for our Australian readers, on a very hot January night.

Ingredients
2	cups black cherries
1	tbsp. honey
1	lemon
4	cups beet borscht*
	sour cream

Preparation
• Stem and seed the cherries.
• Put them in a saucepan, cover them with water, and simmer for 12 minutes.
• Add the honey and the juice of the lemon.
• Strain the borscht, and add the liquid to the cherries mixture.
• Refrigerate until very cold.
• Serve with a dollop of sour cream.

Serves 5 or 6.

---

* You may use the bottled store-bought borscht, or you may follow any standard recipe for cold beet borscht.

"Good yontiff, Pontiff. Would you like my secret recipe for borscht with cherries and honey?"

25

HOT SHERRIED AVOCADO SOUP WITH AVOCADO BALLS THEREIN

Most people don't think about making soup from avocados, which is a pity since they have an unusual and delicate flavor, especially when heated. The flavor, however, tends to go away when they are heated to the boiling point, so be careful when you make this rich and delicious concoction. *Note:* One of our recipe testers reported that while the taste of this was fine, the color was a bit, um, unusual, suggesting that it might be appropriate for a candlelight dinner.

Ingredients

2   medium-sized avocados
4   cups beef stock
3   tbsp. parsley
3   tbsp. sherry
     salt and pepper to taste

Preparation

- Cut one avocado in half, remove the pit, scoop out the meat, and purée it.
- Mince the parsley fine and add it, along with the sherry, salt, and pepper, to the puréed avocado.
- Bring the beef stock to the boiling point, and then let it cool slightly.
- Fold in the avocado mixture, and pour at once into hot bowls.
- Using a melon-baller, make avocado balls from avocado number two, and plop them in the soup as garnish.
- Serve immediately.

Serves 4 to 6

ICED SELTZER-WATER SOUP

This strange concoction is loosely based on what purports to be an Iranian peasant dish, although the availability of, and predilection for, iced sparkling water in Iranian peasant villages must be questioned by the serious culinary scholar. Nevertheless, the soup *is* unusual, extremely refreshing, and just the right thing for lunch on a hot summer day.

Ingredients

1¼ pints yogurt
¼ pint cream
4 tsp. raisins
4 tsp. dill seed or weed
4 tsp. chopped onion
1½ medium cucumbers
3 hard-boiled eggs
    ice-cold soda water

Preparation

• Chop up the raisins, dill, onion, cucumbers, and eggs very fine.
• Stir into the yogurt and cream.
• Add as much soda water as you think looks reasonable just before serving.
  (Start with a cup and go from there.)

Serves 4 to 6.

JERUSALEM ARTICHOKE-SALAMI-GINGER ALE SOUP

This is one of those strange chemical reactions, where all of those crazy ingredients, plus tomatoes and onions, combine unexpectedly to make a most delicious dish. This soup is quite filling, thus is good either for a complete lunch, or preceding a less-substantial main course for dinner.

Ingredients
1   12-ounce can ginger ale (or 1½ cups ginger ale)
2   ginger ale-sized cans of water (3 cups)
1   14.5 ounce can of tomatoes
1   bunch of green onions, cut in ½ inch pieces
¼ pounds thin-sliced salami, cut in ½ inch squares
1   pound Jerusalem artichokes
1   pound celery (6 or 7 large stalks), chopped
1   tsp. basil
1   tsp. oregano
1   bay leaf
1   tsp. rosemary

Preparation
• In a small soup pot, mix together the ginger ale, water, tomatoes, and green onions.
• Add spices and bring to a boil. Simmer for one hour.
• Meanwhile, scrub the Jerusalem artichokes lightly and boil them for 20 minutes in just enough water to cover.
• When they are done, let them cool slightly, peel them, and after the ginger ale has cooked for an hour, add the artichokes along with the celery.
• Simmer another hour, and spoon into large bowls.
• Add the salami and simmer 15 min. Serve.

Serves 6 to 8.

MIXED GREEN SALAD SOUP WITH OIL AND VINEGAR DRESSING

Yes, that's right, soup. This is a soup that was invented as a solution to the problem of a vast amount of leftover mixed green salad with oil and vinegar dressing. But it is sufficiently tasty that we suggest you mix up a big batch of such salad just to make the soup out of. The vinegar provides an interesting and unexpected sub-taste.

Ingredients

1 to 2 cups consommé or chicken broth
1   tbsp. flour
1   very large mixed green salad with oil and vinegar dressing, including, for instance, lettuce, tomatoes, onions, cucumbers, radishes, etc.

Preparation

• Pour 1 cup of the broth or consommé in a blender or food processor.
• Add flour and blend until the flour is dissolved.
• Reserve a heaping cup of salad (for garnish).
• Now pour the salad and dressing into your blender or processor, blending until you have a thick purée.
• Add as much of the second cup of broth as necessary for the consistency you prefer.
• Cook in a double boiler for 30 minutes, covered, stirring occasionally.
• Chop the reserved salad and use as a garnish in the middle of each bowl of Salad Soup.

Serves 6 to 8

PEANUT BOURBON SOUP

This unusual soup may never have been served on the Old Plantation, but it sure tastes like the sort of thing they *would* have served if they had thought of it. The alcohol in the bourbon is cooked away, leaving its flavor only, so you can serve this to minors without endangering their moral fibre.

Ingredients
2	tbsp. butter
½	cup celery, chopped
1	medium onion, chopped
1	tbsp. flour
	pinch of curry powder
4	cups chicken stock
2	tbsp. bourbon
½	cup chunky peanut butter
1	cup milk
¼	cup chopped salted peanuts
	dash of paprika
	(chopped green onion, optional)

Preparation
• Melt the butter in a saucepan over low heat.
• Add the onion and celery to the butter.
• Cook until tender, but not brown.
• Stir in the flour and curry powder until the mixture is smooth.
• Add the chicken stock and bourbon, and bring to a boil.
• Blend in the peanut butter and simmer for 15 minutes.
• Add the milk and heat to just below the boiling point.
• Pour into serving bowls, add a spoonful of chopped peanuts, and sprinkle lightly with paprika (and green onions, if you'd like)

Serves 4 or 5

PUMPKIN CHICKEN SOUP

This soup, amazingly enough, tastes almost exactly like pumpkin-chicken soup should taste. When you serve it, people are likely to say, "Hmmm, this is pumpkin-chicken soup, is it not?" But that doesn't mean they've ever had it before. Almost no one has. Until you prepare it, that is. After which ever-increasing numbers of people probably will, since the stuff tastes so good.

Ingredients

5   tsp. butter
¼   cup minced onions
2   cups canned pumpkin
3   cups chicken broth
½   tsp. salt
1   cup half-and-half
     dash of cayenne pepper
     dash of nutmeg

How to make it

• Melt the butter in a large saucepan.
• Sauté the onions for 5 minutes.
• Stir in the broth, the pumpkin, the salt, and the pepper.
• Bring to a boil, and then cook over low heat for 30 minutes.
• Stir in the half-and-half and reheat, but not to boiling.
• Sprinkle with nutmeg just before serving.

Serves 4 or 5

SEVEN-HOUR MUSHROOM-ONION-BLUE CHEESE SOUP

This simple soup will fill a 73-room house with magnificent smells all day long. Although it cooks for seven hours, it only requires your attention at the start, briefly about half way through, and then again at the end (for purposes of eating). If you have a friend who will come in and add the blue cheese, you could put the soup on, fly from Cincinnati to Boise and back again, arriving just in time to take it off the flame. Fortunately you do not have to.

Ingredients

¼ cup cooking oil
4 garlic cloves
12 medium-sized onions
1 pound mushrooms
12 cups well-flavored beef consommé or stock
½ pound blue cheese
salt and pepper to taste

Preparation

• Coat the inside of a very large pot (at least 6 quarts) with the oil.
• Chop the onions fairly coarsely, the mushrooms mediumly, and the garlic finely,
• Add them all to the pot.
• Add the beefy liquid, then fill the pot to about 2 inches from the top with water.
• Bring to a boil, lower to a simmer and cook for about 4 hours.
• Toss the blue cheese in the pot, and add salt and pepper to taste.
• Fill to near the top again with water and simmer covered, for about three more hours.

Serves 6-8

SIMPLE PEACH SOUP WITH ROSES

A simple peach soup with roses is sort of the culinary equivalent of a simple brooch from Tiffany's, or a simple trip around the world. It may be simple, but it is still exquisite, unusual, and very special.

Ingredients
3   tbsp. sugar
2   tbsp. cornstarch
1   cup cold water
1   tbsp. lard (Yes, you can substitute vegetable shortening.)
½   pound peaches
1   tsp. rose flavoring (rose water, or essence of roses, available in Middle Eastern markets)

Preparation
• Mix the cornstarch and sugar into the water.
• Melt the lard in a saucepan and bring it to a boil.
• Remove the pan from the stove and add the cornstarch-sugar-water mixture to the lard.
• Mix well.
• Continue heating over low heat.
• Peel and de-pit the peaches, and mash them with a fork.
• Add the mashed peaches to the sauce mixture, and cook, stirring constantly, until it boils.
• Add the rose flavoring.
• Serve hot or cold.

Serves 2 or 3

STRING BEAN SOUP WITH TOMATOES ON TOAST

This is a very thick soup, consisting of little more than string beans and tomatoes cooked together. Oh, and served on toast. If it were any thicker, it would be included in the sandwich section under "String Bean and Tomato Sandwiches." Which, come to think of it, isn't such a bad idea.

Ingredients
1 tbsp. olive oil
1 clove garlic, peeled and crushed
2 medium-sized tomatoes
1 pound small green string beans
   salt and pepper to taste
4 slices toast

Preparation
• Peel, deseed, and finely chop the tomatoes.
• Cook them uncovered over very low heat for 20 minutes.
• In a large pot, heat the olive oil and brown the garlic in same.
• Remove the garlic and donate it to charity.
• Add the tomatoes and the beans, season with salt and pepper, add about a cup of hot water, and cook slowly over medium heat until the beans are tender.
• Inspect, taste, and add enough hot water every five minutes or so to keep the consistency at that of a thick soup (or a thin stew).
• Serve over toast in shallow bowls or soup plates.

Serves 4

Official U.S. government photograph entitled "Picking String Beans in Field," taken by Russell Lee near Muskogee, Oklahoma in June, 1939

TOMATO COCONUT SOUP

When Laura McClurg was served this tomato soup on a cruise ship, it was immediately apparent that it was out of the ordinary. The chef would only say that there was a "secret ingredient." Finally she was able to learn (she did not share her methodology with us) that the special ingredient was, in fact, coconut. Here's how you can do it on your yacht or in your kitchen.

Ingredients:
1   large can peeled whole tomatoes
½   tomato can of water
½ to 1 cup of milk
½ to 1 cup of coconut flakes (depending on preference)
     pinch of salt
     pinch of pepper
pinch of sugar or honey (if desired)

Preparation
• Puree tomatoes with juice in blender with water.
• Heat to a slow boil on medium heat in saucepan.
• Stir milk in slowly.
• Bring back to low boil.
• Add coconut, salt, pepper, and sugar.
• Simmer on low for 30-45 minutes, stirring occasionally.

Serves 4

TOMATO SOUP WITH BANANAS

Shortest recipe in the book. But a good one. And one that leaves us enough room to include a big picture of a Mongolian archer that we took last year at Naadam, the big national sports festival in Ulaan Baatar. No, it has nothing to do with this recipe, as best we can tell.

Ingredients
1   bowl tomato soup
1   banana

Preparation
• Slice bananas into soup. Eat.

MAIN DISHES

ALL-DAY TEEPEE TURKEY

This interesting way to prepare a simple turkey was sent to us by Paul Gasparo, who tells us that it is a fine thing to do on a camping trip (assuming you've chosen to lug your turkey along with you, or if you've chosen to camp in the supermarket parking lot), because you can start the cooking early in the day, and it will be ready for a late lunch or an early dinner. The first key to making it work is to wrap your tripod very carefully with several layers of foil. (This refers to the cooking tripod you will build, not your camera, please.) And the second key is to check the coals every hour or two to be sure they are still smouldering. If not, replace them.

Ingredients
1   15 lb. turkey, giblets removed, rinsed, and seasoned to taste
3   empty #10 cans (the big tomato juice type)
     Hammer and nail to make holes in the cans
     Charcoal
     Tripod, built from three large branches, 3 to 4 feet long, tied or wired
        together at the top.
     Wire or string for the tripod, and to hang the turkey
     Heavy duty aluminum foil

Preparation
• Truss the turkey with the wings and legs tight to the body.
• Hang the turkey from the tripod with its legs down, so it is about 18 inches
     from the ground.
• Make 6 to 8 holes in each of the three big cans, at varying heights, with a big
     one or two near the bottom.
• Place one or two sheets of crumpled (but not too tightly) newspaper in the
     bottom of each of the three big cans.
• Fill each can with charcoal.
• Place one can at the base of each pole of the tripod (inside the teepee you are
     making).
• Set fire to the newspaper in each can (through the bottom-most hole).
• Wrap the tripod in foil, from the ground to the very top, at least two layers. This
     should be as airtight as possible.

BAKED MACKEREL

STUFFED WITH GOOSEBERRIES AND EGGS

Do you suppose mackerels on the hoof eat lots of gooseberries and eggs? Well they certainly *should* (tell any mackerels with whom you are on speaking terms), since the combination is excellent.

Ingredients

1   mackerel per person
chopped parsley
butter
5   tbsp. cream
½   pound gooseberries per mackerel
1   hardboiled egg per person (or per mackerel)
salt and pepper to taste

Preparation

• Clean and bone the fish, being careful not to cut the skin.
• Remove the stalks from the gooseberries and boil half of them for 5 minutes in lightly-salted water.
• Remove the skins from all the gooseberries (cooked and raw).
• Place the berries together with the hardboiled eggs, one pinch per person of chopped parsley, of salt, and of pepper, in the bowl of a food processor and blend until it is very finely chopped.
• Stuff each fish with the mixture. Tie fish together with a string at 2 or 3 places, put into a well-buttered dish, pour melted butter over them
• Cook at 350° for 30 minutes, basting frequently.
• 10 minutes before serving, add the cream to the sauce, stir well, and if there was any gooseberry stuffing left over, add it now, too.

Serves as many as you have prepared mackerels.

BEAN ROAST

This amalgam might well be subtitled "What to do when your vegetarian friends are coming to dinner, and you've already served them all the egg and pasta dishes in your repertoire." So much vegetarian cookery seems designed to imitate some sort of meat dish as closely as possible without actually using meat. This is something else. It's smooth, sweet, and spicy. We actually do suggest using a wee bit of bacon fat, but if you wish to remain purist, take off your leather shoes, and substitute butter or margarine. And please try not to think about how green peppers are supposed to scream silently when plucked from the vine.

Ingredients

2   tbsp. minced green pepper
2   tbsp. minced onion
2   tbsp. butter, margarine or bacon fat
4   cups canned baked beans, well drained and mashed
2   eggs
2   cups soft bread crumbs—the kind you make by crumbling or mincing toast
or slightly stale bread rather than the dry boxed variety of breadcrumbs
1   can (14.5 oz.) diced tomatoes, drained
       salt, freshly-ground pepper and paprika

Preparation

• Brown the pepper and onion in the fat.
• Add beans, slightly beaten eggs, bread crumbs, and tomatoes.
• Season with salt, pepper, and paprika. (Unfortunately you have to guess here, because we don't recommend tasting the mixture with raw egg in it. Try a teaspoon of sweet Hungarian paprika.)
• Stir gently.
• Pack in greased baking dish or meatloaf pan and cook uncovered for one hour at 325°

Serves 6 to 8

P.S. Next day you can make patties of the leftover loaf, if there is any. Coat them with dried breadcrumbs, sauté until browned in butter or oil, and serve with salsa and a dab of guacamole. Almost worth making this just for the leftovers.

BEEF FOR 1,000 (OR FEWER) COOKED FOR 12 HOURS IN A HOLE IN THE GROUND

Recipe-reducing is supposed to be quite an art. That is, if a recipe makes 8 servings and you only want 3 servings, you probably need a computer and a degree in mathematics to figure out what to do. Of course if you were to practice more, you might become better at this. Here is a recipe for you to practice on.

Ingredients

500 pounds beef, cut into 25 pound pieces
10 pounds salt
40 yards of cheesecloth
   stout twine
100 pounds dry sand
60 square feet of sheet metal
1 shovel

We're hungry!

Preparation

• Remove all bones from the beef.
• Tie each piece up in a large roll, using stout twine.
• Salt each piece (half a pound per piece) and wrap it up in cheesecloth.
• Dig a pit 5 feet deep, 3 feet wide, and 20 feet long.
• Build a huge wood fire in the pit, such that the top is about a foot from the ground.
• Let the fire burn until the coals are glowing.
• Cover the coals with a thin layer of fine dry sand.
• Place the beef on the sand, cover with the sheet metal, and fill the hole with dirt, to ground level.
• Cook for 12 hours.

Serves 1,000, give or take a few.

Note: All right, you *can* make this in a somewhat more modest volume. Consider 10 pounds of beef, ¼ pound of salt, and a 2-foot deep hole, into which you've put charcoal briquettes (which you might want to start on your barbecue). In lieu of sheet metal, you could use a large cookie sheet or two. This version would serve 18 to 20.

BEEF LIVER
SOAKED IN BRINE FOR TWO WEEKS, HUNG FROM THE CEILING FOR 2 WEEKS, AND STORED IN THE CLOSET FOR 22 WEEKS

(see page 12)

People don't cure liver much any more—if, in fact, they ever did—because there is so much effort involved. Also, there is the possible embarrassment of having liver hanging from your ceiling for two weeks. ("What's that, a new chandelier?" "Well, no. As a matter of fact, it's a beef liver." "A bee flivver?" "No, you see . . . .") But some people agree that it is all worth the effort, in the end. When cooked at last, the taste is subtle, delicate, and most unusual.

Ingredients

1 large beef liver	newspaper
pinch of saltpeter (potassium nitrate)	string
salt	

How to make it

- Cut the liver into 2 or 3 pieces.
- Add enough salt to a big jar or crock of water so that a whole egg will float in it.
- Remove the egg; it was just to test saltiness.
- Add saltpeter.
- Soak the liver for two weeks.
- Remove, and hang from the ceiling by string until it is absolutely and totally dried out—about two weeks.
- Then wrap it in newspapers, tightly, and store in a cool dark place (like a closet or basement) for about 4 months.
- To prepare, cut into thin slices, and sauté in half butter, half cream until the liver curls up.

Note: Saltpeter is available at many drugstores. If you notice smiles when you ask for it, that may be because it is a legendary, if never proven, anaphrodisiac: something reputedly put into the food at boarding schools to cause the young men to think about math and history rather than girls and girls.

CAJUN JOE'S TRASHCAN TURKEY

Our internet quest for unusual recipes yielded this one, sent to us by "CajunLou" who got it from "CajunJoe," and we gratefully thank them both. If the Teepee Turkey on page 37 was a little too wild for you, here's a variation you can do in the backyard.

Ingredients

    10 gallon galvanized garbage pail
    2" x 2" wooden stake---2 ft. long
10   pounds. charcoal briquettes
    Heavy duty aluminum foil--18" wide
10-12½ pound turkey, thawed, washed, and dried. You can inject it with marinade, if you want, but do rub it with oil or butter flavored Crisco and coat with Cajun seasoning.
1 shovel

Preparation

• Clear a circle of ground about 3 feet across. Dump the charcoal in the middle.
• Light entire 10 pounds of charcoal in a pile and let burn for about 20 minutes, until white.
• While coals are heating, drive stake into ground, leaving about 12" extending above ground. Wrap stake with aluminum foil. Spread additional foil on ground around stake to make an area about 3 ft.
• Place turkey on stake through open butt end with neck up.
• Invert trash can over turkey. Make sure top and sides of container *do not* touch bird.
• Shovel one layer of burning coals over top area of trash can. Shovel remainder of coals evenly around base of can, touching can all the way around.
• Let cook 90 minutes undisturbed.
• Carefully remove hot ashes from top and sides of can. Lift off can carefully. Take its temperature (185° is done). Remove turkey from stake.
• Carve and serve.

CHEESEBURGER AND A CUPPA COFFEE
BAKED IN A PIE

Which, you may admit, is nearly as interesting as four and twenty black birds, for which we were unable to find a suitable recipe. All to the good, we suppose; what do you suppose the reaction would be if you asked the lady at the supermarket poultry counter for twenty-four small black birds, please.

Ingredients

2½   pounds very lean hamburger meat
2   cups soft whole wheat bread crumbs
2   eggs
½   cup strong coffee
½   cup evaporated milk
1   small onion, grated or processed very fine
2   tsp. meat tenderizer or MSG*
1   tsp. Worcestershire sauce
1   tbsp. prepared mustard
4   slices of cheese: either American or cheddar, as you wish

Preparation

• Mix the meat, bread crumbs, and eggs together.
• Mix the coffee, milk, and onion together.
• Let the two mixtures stand separately for 10 minutes, then mix them together, along with the tenderizer, Worcestershire, and mustard.
• Pat the mixture into an even layer in a 10-inch pie plate.
• Bake at 350° for one hour.
• Cut the cheese slices in half diagonally, and arrange around the outside edge of the pie.
• Broil until the cheese melts and turns brown.

Serves 6 to 8

---

* Yes, we know that MSG got a really bad rap in the press—"Chinese restaurant syndrome" and all—but we are persuaded by a lot of more recent evidence that MSG is quite all right, after all.

CHICKEN COOKED ON A BEER CAN

We're not sure what kind of doctor Dr. Vicky Campagna is, but she certainly knows how to doctor a chicken in a most innovative fashion, as in this clever approach she shared with us, replacing an expensive vertical roasting device with a simple hot beer can. A *very* hot beer can, so be careful when you remove the chicken + can apparatus from the grill.

Ingredients

1   can of beer (12 ounces)
½   cup barbecue sauce
1   tbsp. dried basil
2   tsp. paprika
¾   tsp. salt
½   tsp. onion powder
¼   tsp. garlic powder
¼   tsp. black pepper
1   chicken -- (3 to 3½ pounds)

Preparation

• Preheat barbecue grill to medium-high heat.
• Empty one half of the beer from can. (You may empty it into yourself if you wish.)
• Fill the now-half-empty beer can with barbecue sauce
• In a small bowl, combine basil, paprika, salt, onion powder, garlic powder and black pepper; mix well.
• Rub this spice mixture evenly over chicken.
• Don't think too closely about the imagery as you lower the cavity of the chicken over the beer can. In other words, the chicken is sitting on the can, as it were.
• Place the chicken and can on the rack in the center of the grill.
• Cover and cook 1 to 1¼ hours, or until chicken is done (internal temperature of 190° should do it).
• Serve with the now-hot sauce from the can.

This is not a 'still' from the movie "Invasion of the Chicken Monsters," but an actual photo of the dish in process.

CHICKEN WITH 23 CLOVES OF GARLIC

Sometimes it is the case that a little bit of something is good, a lot of it is not so good, but then, unexpectedly, a vast amount of it is good again. This is what happens with the garlic in this unusual chicken dish. One or two cloves would be normal; 5 or 6 cloves would be too much garlic. But when you put 23 cloves of garlic in the pot, something new and wonderful happens.

Ingredients

1	chicken
23	cloves garlic
5	tsp. oil
1	tsp. cognac
½	tsp. tarragon
¼	tsp. nutmeg
1	bay leaf
½	tsp. thyme
½	tsp. parsley
	salt and pepper to taste

Preparation

• Arrange all the herbs except the nutmeg in the bottom of a pot.

• Peel the 23 cloves of garlic and put them on top of the herbs.

• Cut the chicken into large pieces, dampen them with the oil, and place on top of the garlic.

• Add salt, pepper, and nutmeg.

• Cover and cook for 50 minutes, adding a bit of warm water from time to time, if it seems too dry inside.

• 15 minutes before serving, add the cognac.

• Serve the chicken on rice or noodles, with the sauce in an adjacent bowl.

Serves 3 to 5

CHOCOLATE CHEESE CHICKEN NICOLE

The three best things about Michigan State University, at the time John earned his Ph.D., there, were the Department of Communications, the football team, and, best of all the campus Dairy Store, where students in the Dairy Sciences Department were able to sell their inventions and creations. Foremost among these, and reason enough to attend State, was their chocolate cheese. The wonderful news, discovered for us by Nicole Ballard, also an MSU alum (and, as it happens, an administrator at the school where Marina earned one of her two Master's degrees)* is that not only is chocolate cheese still being made, it can be purchased by mail, at the bargain price (in 2002) of $4.32 per pound. Purchase information on page 136. The rest of the world is just beginning to discover this wonder. It was the First Place Winner at the Michigan State Fair in the processed cheese category in both 2000 and 2001. We didn't make the Rose Bowl, but we have this to fall back upon. And Nicole, who knows her way around a kitchen as well as a campus, has created two intriguing recipes using chocolate cheese. Here's one; the other can be found on page 136. *Warning:* This does not keep well. It is fine hot the first time, but the leftovers looked pretty dreadful (yet tasted OK) when they spent a night in the refrigerator.

Ingredients

6	medium chicken breasts	1	tsp. ground lemon pepper
3	tbsp. grape seed oil	1	tsp. ground allspice
1	28 oz. can of whole stewed or plum tomatoes	3	bay leaves
12	medium peperoncini, sliced, with seeds	8	ounces chocolate cheese, cubed
2	tbsp. pinenuts, coarsely chopped	½	cup pesto sauce

Preparation

• Brown chicken breasts in oil.
• Place in baking dish, reserving oil. Place dish in a 350 degree oven.
• Empty tomatoes into medium sauce pan, heating over low heat. Gently stir in oil from chicken, pesto, pinenuts, spices, peperoncini, and bay leaves.
• Continue stirring, breaking tomatoes apart, until mixture bubbles gently.
• Add chocolate cheese, stirring until cheese has melted into sauce.
• Remove chicken from oven and pour the sauce over it.
• Return dish to the oven and continue baking an additional 30 minutes.
• Serve over rice. Serves 6.

_____

* California State University, Dominguez Hills, where the M.A. in Humanities can be earned entirely by distance learning. http://www.csudh.edu

CHOCOLATE CHILI WITH CORNFLAKES

The Native Americans, and subsequently the Spanish, learned long ago that bitter chocolate is a very good flavoring for meat dishes. Other people have been much slower to discover this, but perhaps dishes like Chocolate Chili will hasten the process. For goodness sake, be sure you don't use sweet or semi-sweet chocolate. We know someone who did, and now, even after his digestive system had recovered, he still shudders whenever he comes within 20 paces of a Holloway Milk Dud.

Ingredients

2	tbsp. butter	4	tbsp. sugar
4	medium onions	2	ounces bitter chocolate
2	cloves garlic	4	tsp. salt
2	tbsp. cumin	2	tbsp. oil
2	tbsp. coriander	1	pound lean ground beef
2	tbsp. oregano	1	egg
2	large cans Italian tomatoes	¾	cup crushed cornflakes
2	cups water	1	can kidney beans (optional)
2	tbsp. chili powder		

Preparation

• Chop the onions and garlic, and brown them in butter.
• Add cumin, coriander, oregano, tomatoes, water, and chili powder.
• Simmer for 5 minutes.
• Add sugar, chocolate, and salt.
• Cook over low heat, covered, for one hour.
• Make meatballs (small ones) from beef, egg, 1 tsp. salt, and cornflakes.
• Brown in oil.
• Add meatballs and beans (if you want them) to sauce.
• Cover and cook one more hour over low heat.
• Serve over rice.

Serves about 4

COFFEED LAMB

Someone—more likely a coffee-lover than a lamb-lover—discovered that coffee and lamb go together more interestingly than many pairs of things. Here is an extremely simple recipe which will enable you to demonstrate this for yourself.

Ingredients

1   6-to-7-pound leg of lamb
2   lemons
4   cups double-strength coffee
4   tbsp. instant coffee
     salt and pepper to taste

Preparation

• Cut 1 lemon in half and rub lamb with it.
• Sprinkle lamb with salt and pepper.
• Put lamb on rack in pan, skin side up.
• Sprinkle the top with instant coffee.
• Slice the second lemon into very thin slices and arrange these on the coffee. (You can anchor them with toothpicks, if need be.)
• Roast at 300º for 30 minutes per pound (for medium lamb). For the last hour of cooking, baste every 15 minutes with the double-strength coffee.

Serves 8 or more.

CORNED WHATEVER
(CORNED BEEF, CORNED PORK, CORNED DEER, CORNED ETC.)

(see page 12)

Corned beef (etc.) in a book like this? Well, yes, since you are going to corn it all by yourself. We think you will find, as all of us corners have found, that self-corned beef somehow tastes far superior to the store-bought variety. And once you have made your corning juice (perhaps in Corning glassware), you can corn practically anything that will hold still. You can even corn several kinds of meat at one time if your crock is big enough.

Most store-bought corned beef is made from brisket. You may find that using a better cut of meat, even steak, will result in an even tastier product.

Ingredients

4	ounces sugar	1½	tsp. sodium nitrate (from a drug store)
2	tbsp. pickling spice	1½	tsp. sodium nitrite (from a drug store)
1	medium onion	4	cloves garlic
3	tsp. black pepper	3 to 8	pounds of salt (see table below)
1	tsp. ground cloves	5	pounds meat for corning (beef, pork, deer game, etc.)
6	bay leaves		
4	quarts water		

Preparation:

- Identify a cold, dark place in which to corn your meat. On our planet, it is commonly called a "refrigerator."
- Dissolve the salt, sugar, nitrate and nitrate in water (heating it as needed)
- Let the water cool.
- Put the water in a big crock along with all the other ingredients. If the meat bobs up, put a plate on top and put a weight on the plate.
- Put the crock in the refrigerator.
- Stir the liquid on the 5th and 10th days, turning the meat around at the same time.
- Remove after 15 days, drain, and either store or cook. Store in refrigerator. Cook by putting in water, bringing to a boil, removing scum from the water, and simmering, covered, for 5 hours.

Serves 6 to 8

CROWN ROAST OF HOT DOG

Silly. Silly, silly, silly. One of the two silliest recipes in this entire book (the other being the Shrimp Christmas Tree on page 21). Crown roast of hot dogs indeed. Actually it tastes just fine; it's just the idea of the thing. Silly. That's what it is. You can see it in all its glory on page 2 of this book.

Ingredients
2	medium onions
2	carrots
2	cups raw spinach
1	small green pepper
3	large stalks celery
4	sprigs parsley

1	egg
2	tbsp. butter
½	cup milk
1	cup dry bread crumbs
18	hot dogs
4 or 5 strips bacon	

Ingredients for the sauce
1	medium onion, diced
½	cup celery, chopped
2	tbsp. butter
4	tbsp. lemon juice
1	tbsp. Worcestershire sauce

1	tsp. mustard
2	tbsp. brown sugar
2	tbsp. vinegar
1	cup ketchup
¼	cup water

Preparation of the Crown Roast
• Chop the vegetables very fine.
• Sauté in butter for about 5 to 7 minutes.
• Add egg (beaten), bread crumbs, salt, pepper, and milk. Consistency should be moist, like turkey stuffing. In fact, if you wish, use stuffing mix here.
• Mold the stuffing into a mound, and stand the hot dogs up around the outside. Skewer the hot dogs into the dressing with bamboo skewers.
• Bake for 20 minutes at 425°.
• Now wrap the bacon around the outside of the roast, impaling it on the toothpicks, and return to the oven until the bacon is cooked, about 10 to 15 minutes. Top with sauce and serve.

Preparation of the sauce
• Cook celery and onion in the butter until soft.
• Add everything else and simmer, uncovered, until hot and slightly thickened.

Serves 8 or so

DRUNKEN TROUT

Trout are rarely found swimming around in streams of Scotch whiskey, but those two flavors do go awfully well together, as demonstrated by this recipe, found for us by Marie Elena Monaco in Michele Evans' excellent book, *Easy Seafood Recipes.** You'll probably want to serve it with fresh green vegetables, salad, and other healthy things, to take your mind off the rather rich ingredients that are used to prepare the fish.

Ingredients

4 small trout cleaned (It also works with larger trout, but this is fancier)
7 tbsp. butter
2 cups cooked rice
¼ pound mushrooms, chopped fine
1 tbsp. chopped parsley
¼ tsp. thyme
½ tsp. salt
½ cup heavy cream
3 tbsp. Scotch whiskey

Preparation

• Sauté trout in 4 tbsp. butter until lightly browned.
• Make 4 sheets of aluminum foil large enough to hold one trout and stuffing. Place each trout on a sheet of foil.
• In a separate pan, sauté mushrooms in 3 tbsp. butter over medium heat. They'll go juicy. Keep sauteing until most of the juice has evaporated.
• Into the mushrooms, stir the cooked rice, parsley, thyme, salt, and pepper.
• Divide this stuffing mix in four portions and place over the trout.
• Pour the heavy cream and Scotch into the skillet where the trout cooked, and bring just to the boiling point.
• Pour equally over the rice mixture.
• Seal the foil over each trout plus mixture.
• Bake in a pan in a preheated 400° oven for about 15 minutes.
• Place the foil packages on each dinner plate for serving.

Serves 4

---

* Published by Dell in 1975, long out-of-print, but we found plenty of used copies for sale on the excellent website called www.bookfinder.com.

FEATHERED HEN COOKED IN CLAY IN A HOLE IN THE GROUND

(see page 12)

It is important, in this odd dish, that the feathers and skin be left on the chicken when the clay is applied. Otherwise the hardened clay will stick to the chicken meat, and you wouldn't want hardened clay sticking to *your* chicken meat. It is an even bet whether you will have more trouble finding the clay or the feathered chicken. Try an art supply store for the former, and an Oriental grocery or a friendly butcher shop for the latter.

Ingredients

1	large hen (5 to 6 pounds), with feathers, but without head or giblets	1	cup of cooked rice
2	green onions, cut in 1" pieces	1	needle
1	tbsp. freshly grated ginger	1	piece of strong thread
1	tsp. sugar	8 to 10	pounds of clay
4	tbsp. soy sauce	1	tsp. white wine
1	tbsp. flour		lots of charcoal

Preparation

• Mix together the onion, ginger, sugar, soy sauce, and wine.
• Stuff the chicken with this. Sew up the chicken, and seal the seam with a paste of flour and water.
• Cover the entire chicken with a layer of clay about two inches thick.
• Now dig a hole about two feet square and two feet deep. (If you live in a city apartment, please do *not* try this recipe.)
• Add enough charcoal to make a pile about 16 inches high. (Either set it ablaze elsewhere, or use the "self-igniting" match-light sort.)
• When the charcoal is glowing, place the encased chicken on the coals, and fill the hole in with dirt. Cook for about two hours. (An ear to the ground is likely to detect a sizzling sound.)
• Remove the now-hardened object from the hole, and wait until the clay cools enough to touch with the bare hand.
• Tap the clay lightly with a hammer until it cracks, and remove it with your hands. The feathers and skin will (you fervently hope, and so do we) stick to the clay. All of them.
• Add one cup of cooked rice to the stuffing. Serve the chicken and stuffing hot.

Serves 6 to 8

FLAMING MEATBALLS IN WALNUTS AND JUNIPER BUTTER

Looky there, Harry, the meatballs caught fire," your guests are apt to say when you bring in this spectacular yet simple creation. Since the brandy definitely flavors the meat, it makes sense, for this dish, to use a very good quality brandy—the sort you'd be willing to drink straight from the snifter.

Ingredients

2   pounds ground tenderloin tips
¼   cup good brandy
2   egg yolks
1   cup cooked wild rice
    salt and pepper to taste
⅔   cup finely-ground walnuts
4   juniper berries
¼   cup sweet butter

Preparation

• With your hands, mix together the meat, egg yolks, cooked rice, salt, and pepper.
• Roll into small meatballs—about 40 to 50 of them. (Dip your fingers into cool water from time to time if the mixture seems to stick to your hands.)
• Roll the meatballs in the walnuts.
• Melt the butter in a saucepan, add the juniper berries, and sauté the meatballs until done, in batches if necessary.
• Place meatballs in a preheated chafing dish.
• Heat the remaining brandy, set fire to same, pour over meatballs, and serve.

Serves 4 to 6

"Egad! Lord Sneedby's meatball seems to have caught fire!"

FLOUNDER WITH BANANAS, ALMONDS, AND RUM

The Black Dog is a restaurant, general store and mail order (and online) emporium on Cape Cod (see www.TheBlackDog.com). (How can you not love a place that features the "Huey, Louie And0ouille Omelet.") Their own excellent cookbook (*Black Dog Summer on the Vineyard*) is published by Little Brown.

Faithful correspondent Marie Elena Monaco found this interesting recipe on their website. She reports that "I tried it. I loved it. My husband and kids hated it." As John's grandmother said, "Go figure."

Ingredients

1	cup flour
½	tsp. salt
¼	tsp. pepper
2	pounds flounder fillets (sole or red snapper fillets work well, too)
2	eggs, beaten
2	tbsp. canola oil
1	tbsp. butter

Ingredients for Rum Bananas

¼ to ½	cup sliced almonds
2	ripe bananas, sliced
¼	cup rum (light or dark)
2	tbsp. butter
	pinch of ground nutmeg
	salt and pepper to taste

Preparation

- Mix flour with salt and pepper in a wide shallow dish.
- Dredge flounder in the flour, shake off the excess, then dip in the beaten egg.
- Combine butter and oil in a sauté pan, and bring to sizzling hot.
- Add fish and sauté quickly, 2 or 3 minutes per side.
- Remove from pan and set on a serving dish in a warm oven.
- To the same pan, add almonds and sauté briefly, just until they begin to brown.
- Add banana slices.
- Now hold the pan away from the heat and add the rum.
- Return pan to heat, add butter and nutmeg, and adjust seasoning.
- Cook 2 minutes more, gently turning the banana slices.
- Turn the banana slices out onto the fish and serve.

Serves 4 to 6

FRIED CHICKEN WITH CHRYSANTHEMUM PETALS
COOKED FOR PRECISELY 1.8 SECONDS

As everyone who eats flowers regularly knows, you can't cook a chrysanthemum for more than two seconds without it turning bitter. Sometimes this is all right, but in this recipe it isn't. Still, you don't want to cook it for less than 1.5 seconds, or it won't l properly cooked. You thus have the choice of buying $700 electronic chrysanthemum cooker, or trying our sin plified method and hoping for the best.

Our simplified method: We analyzed dozens of wo combinations, and found that one thing nearly everyor 1.8 seconds to say is "St. Louis, Missouri." So when it comes time to cook your chrysanthemum petals, fling them in the pot, say "St. Louis, Missouri" at your normal speaking rate, and take the pot off the fire. If they taste bitter, you talk too slowly.

Ingredients

¾ pound cooked white chicken meat
1½ tbsp. cornstarch
1 tsp. salt
2 tbsp. peanut oil
1 tsp. chopped green onion
1 tsp. minced ginger root

1 tbsp. sherry
1½ tsp. sugar
1 cup water
   petals from 30 small white
     chrysanthemums
1 tsp. sesame oil

Preparation

• Cut the chicken into thin slices, as for julienne.
• Dust with 1 tbsp. of cornstarch, and sprinkle with salt.
• Heat the oil. Add the chicken and stir fry for 30 seconds..
• Add the ginger and onion and fry for 2 minutes over medium heat.
• Dissolve the remaining ½ tablespoon of cornstarch in the sherry.
• Dissolve the sugar in the water.
• Add both mixtures to the chicken and cook until the sauce thickens.
• Now add the sesame oil and the chrysanthemum petals ("St. Louis, Missouri"), remove from heat, toss lightly together, and serve immediately.

Serves 2

GIGANTIC LAMB PICKLE

Our dear, late friend, Jim Campbell, longtime professor of business at Wichita State University, invented the lamb pickle. If, he reasoned in his scholarly way, you can pickle cucumbers, tomatoes, watermelon rind, and suchlike, why not make a lamb pickle. And so he did. It is so delicious that even now, years after the creation, scores of people in Wichita and the surrounding area are probably wandering around in a giant-lamb-pickle-induced stupor. And so may you. Note: You will need to think ahead—it takes a week to pickle a lamb.

Ingredients

6	pound leg of lamb
6	cups burgundy
1½	cups red wine vinegar
¼	cup gin
1	large yellow onion in thick slices
6	large carrots, in 2" pieces
2	large stalks celery, in 1" pieces

1	clove garlic
¼	tsp. sage
1	bay leaf
2	tsp. salt
1	tsp. pepper
1	cup olive oil
½	cup butter
¼	tsp. tarragon

Ingredients for the special sauce

4	cups beef stock
½	cup red wine
½	cup chopped onion

½	cup red currant jelly
½	cup chopped carrot
½	cup chopped celery
4	tbsp. cornstarch

Preparation of the lamb pickle

- Make the marinade by mixing together the burgundy, vinegar and gin.
- Sauté the onion along with carrots and celery, in the ½ cup of olive oil for 5 minutes. Do not drain, but add to marinade along with the herbs, salt and pepper.
- Insert lamb in the marinade and refrigerate.
- Baste two to four times a day (or whenever you think of it, which we assure you will be at least that often). Do this for eight days.
- When pickled (the lamb, we mean), drain it thoroughly, reserving the marinate, and pat dry with paper towels.

Preheat the oven to 475°. Cook the lamb for 20 minutes, basting it every 4 minutes with a mixture of ½ cup melted butter and ½ cup olive oil. Then add the vegetables from the marinade and roast until your meat thermometer reads 145°—roughly an hour and a quarter.

- Meanwhile, make the special sauce.

The Special Sauce
- Bring the beef stock and red wine to a boil in a sauce pan.
- Filch the following from the lamb: ½ cup each of carrots, onions, and celery.
- Dice the roasted vegetables and add.
- Simmer for 20 minutes.
- Add 1 cup of strained marinade.
- Take 1 tbsp. of sauce liquid for each cup of sauce you have, and cool it.
- Add cornstarch to the cooled liquid and return it to the sauce.
- Heat to boiling point, and add the current jelly.
- Cook over medium heat, stirring, until thickened.
- Serve with lamb pickle.

Serves 6 to 8, with leftovers

GLAZED FLAMING BOURBONED HAM STUFFED WITH FRUITCAKE

You say you're not satisfied merely with a flaming ham? You say you want more than just a glazed bourboned flaming ham? All right, then, how about a glazed, flaming, bourboned ham stuffed with fruitcake. Will that do? Good. Just be sure you get a *bone-in* ham, not a *boneless* ham.

Ingredients
1   10-12 pound ready-to-eat bone-in ham, with the bone removed
¾   cup bourbon
3 or 4 cups fruitcake
½   cup chopped walnuts
¼   cup sugar

Preparation
• Preheat the oven to 350º.
• Crumble the fruitcake and mix with the walnuts.
• Put 2 tablespoons of bourbon and a quarter of the fruitcake into a food processor or blender and blend until finely chopped.
• Repeat with more bourbon and more fruitcake until all of both are blended together.
• Stuff the ham (the cavity where the bone was) with this mixture, and tie it up with a string.
• Wrap in foil and place on a rack in a roasting pan.
• Bake for 12 minutes per pound (roughly two hours total).
• Remove from the oven and tear away the foil.
• Sprinkle with sugar and put back in a 500º oven for 5 minutes to glaze.
• Remove the string. Place ham on a platter. Call everybody into the kitchen.
• Heat ¼ cup bourbon until it flames, and pour over the ham.
• Cut into thin slices and serve.

Serves about 16 people, depending on their size, and the ham's.

HAM AND YAM AND BANANA MANNA

This dish is unusual for reasons other than that the name of it has no vowels other than A.* The hot bananas add just the right touch to transform an otherwise fairly straightforward hammy stew into a real treat.

Ingredients

4   pounds smoked ham hocks
2   quarts water
1   large onion
5   cloves
¼   tsp. thyme
¼   tsp. pepper
3   medium white potatoes
3   medium yams or sweet potatoes
4   ripe bananas
½   cup sliced green onions

Preparation

• Have the butcher (or the spouse) saw the hamhocks into 2 or 3 pieces each.
• Pour the water (cold) over the ham.
• Stud the onion with cloves, and add to the pot along with thyme and pepper.
• Heat, covered, to boiling, and then simmer for 1¼ hours.
• Add the potatoes or yams and simmer 45 minutes longer.
• Remove from heat and let stand 15 minutes to allow the fat to rise.
• Skim off the fat on top and add salt if it needs some.
• Peel and cut the bananas into 2-inch lengths, and add to the pot along with the green onions.
• Simmer for 7 minutes longer, and serve. (You can either serve the ham on a plate and the rest in a bowl, or put the whole works in a big bowl.)
• This is very good with rice.

Serves 5 or 6

---

* Do you suppose there would be a market for a cookbook where "a" was the only vowel? Probably no sillier than some that are out there now. Let's see, there would be Alaska clam jam, Alabama lamb salsa, ham hash, yam salad. OK, we'll stop now.

(see page 12)

HAM COOKED BY BEING SUSPENDED IN THE FIREPLACE FOR 6 MONTHS

If you have a wood-burning fireplace, and if you use it during the winter, you can make a magnificent smoked ham all by yourself. You don't have to worry about using the fireplace every day. As long as you use it once or twice a week during the winter, your ham will be luscious and ready for eating by the first day of spring.

Ingredients

1 12-15 pound raw ham
2 pounds of salt
4 oz. black pepper

1 cement nail
   burlap bag
2 "S" hooks + link chain
   sifted wood ashes

Preparation

• On the first day of autumn, or thereabouts, buy the ham.
• Mix together 1 pound of salt, the pepper, and the sifted wood ashes.
• Rub about one fifth of this mixture onto the ham.
• Store the ham in a cool place. Every 3 days, bring it out, wipe off the ashes with a dry rag, and recoat with more of the ash-salt-pepper mixture. Do this five times, a total of 15 days.
• Now, wash and rinse the burlap bag well.
• Boil it for 10 minutes in a pot with the water and the remaining pound of salt.
• Remove from heat and allow to cool.
• Remove the bag from the cool water, wring out, and allow to dry in the sun. When it is dry, place the ham inside, tie the top securely shut, and store in the same cool place for two more weeks.
• Next, buy a length of link chain that will reach from the top of your chimney to three feet above the middle of the fire. Hammer the cement nail into the top of the chimney, fasten one S-hook to each end of the chain, fasten one end of the chain to the ham and the other to the cement nail, and lower the chain and ham down the chimney.
• Have a lovely winter.
• On the first day of spring, or thereabouts, haul the ham back up the chimney.
• Remove the now-blackened burlap, and wash the ham with a mixture of warm water and baking soda. The ham is now thoroughly cooked, and may be eaten with no further preparation. The only "problem" with this recipe is that you'll have to wait a whole year for the next crop.

HOME-PRESSED BEEF WITH RED WINE JELLY

This recipe sounds awfully complicated, but it is not. It is merely lengthy, and well worth it. Very few people press their own beef any more (and there's nothing worse than a wrinkled beef!). Feel proud when you serve up this luscious dish the day after tomorrow (it takes a day and a half to make), when you can point to the meat and say, "I pressed it m'self!"

Ingredients

5	pounds short ribs of beef	1	veal knuckle
1	celery stalk	3	cups dry red wine
2	medium onions	3	garlic cloves
2	cloves	2	bay leaves
1½	tsp. salt	½	tsp. Worcestershire sauce
3	dashes Tabasco sauce	1	egg

Preparation

• Put all the ingredients *except* the egg into a big pot and cook gently, uncovered, for 4 hours.
• Pull the bones from the meat, and set the meat aside in a big bowl.
• Strain what remains, and clarify the broth as per the next six steps:
• Mix 1 egg white with 1 tsp. cold water.
• Crush the eggshell and add.
• Pour this mixture into the broth and heat to boiling, stirring constantly.
• Simmer 3 minutes.
• Turn off the heat and let it sit on the stove for 20 minutes.
• Strain through a sieve lined with two layers of cheesecloth, and what comes through is clarified broth.
• Simmer the clarified broth until only one cup remains.
• Pour this over the meat.
• Rig something up to press down on the meat. Two suggestions: Keep the meat in a big bowl; take a smaller bowl that fits into the big bowl, rest it on the meat, and put lots of heavy stuff (books, fishing weights, your dog) into the smaller bowl. Or, if you have a canister set, put the meat in a big canister, and put a smaller canister inside the larger one, filling the smaller one with heavy stuff.
• Refrigerate this overnight. Serve cold the next day.

Serves ___

HONEY LAMB WITH SOY SAUCE

The honey with which you smear the lamb not only seems to seal in the lamb juices, but it also imparts a most delicious flavor, which blends admirably with the flavor of the soy sauce with which you baste it.

Ingredients
1   leg of lamb
     honey
1   cup soy sauce
     cornstarch
     salt and pepper to taste

Preparation
• Cut as much fat as you can off the lamb.
• Rub all over with pepper and salt lightly.
• Smear thickly all over with honey.
• Place ¼ inch of water in the bottom of a baking pan, put the lamb in, and pour the soy sauce over same.
• Bake for 30 minutes at 425°, and then at 350° until done (at 30 minutes per pound total). Baste frequently.
• Dissolve some cornstarch in cold water and add to the gravy to thicken it, if you wish.
• Put Al Jolson recording of "My Honey Lamb" on the turntable, and dine.

This is actually a honey dispenser shaped like a lamb. The things one finds on an internet search!

HOT BUTTERED SPAGHETTI TOPPED WITH HOT BUTTERED PEAS

So simple, and so delicious, it's a wonder no one ever thought of it before. Or if they did, then why didn't anyone tell us, since we are among the twenty most prodigious spaghetti-eaters in the northern hemisphere.

Ingredients

    spaghetti
    peas (preferably fresh; otherwise frozen; *not* canned)
    butter
    parmesan cheese (optional)

Preparation

- A. Cook spaghetti.
- B. Cook peas.
- C. Drain spaghetti.
- D. Drain peas.
- E. Melt butter into spaghetti.
- F. Melt butter into peas.
- G. Pour item B onto item A (perhaps sprinkle with PC) and insert into item M (mouth).

HOT ROCK CHICKEN

Paul Gasparo must be a fun guy to go camping with. He has shared a number of nifty and unusual ways to prepare tasty food while on a camping trip (or even in your own back yard), including this method for roasting a chicken making use of nothing more than eight hot rocks and some foil.

Ingredients

1   chicken
8   round rocks, each approximately the size of a chicken egg
        Herbs and spices
        Foil
        Tongs

Preparation

• About six hours before you want to eat, take those eight round rocks and put them in the camp fire.
• Leave them there for about two hours.
• Meanwhile, season your chicken as you wish.
• When the rocks are really hot, using tongs, place one rock under each wing and thigh place (that's the technical anatomical term: "wing and thigh place"), and the remainder inside the chicken.
• Wrap tightly in two or three layers of foil.
• You can actually put this steaming fowl in your backpack, or leave it behind where the bears and ants won't get at it. Either way, in about four hours, you'll have a nicely cooked chicken, ready to eat. But to be safe, please take a thermometer along, and make sure the inside of your chicken is at 190°.

Serves 4

The above illustration is not an authentic or even extant object, nor is there anything really called the "Hot Rock Cafe." There is, however, an excellent "Hard Rock Cafe," and its merchandise can be acquired here: http://www.hardrock.com/

LOCO MOCO A LA HILO

In the early 1990s, we had the pleasure (well, some of it was a pleasure) of living in Hilo, on the Big Island of Hawaii, the place that eats more Spam per capita than anywhere on earth. Spam did not top our family taste charts, and we did not develop an affinity for poi, so the only important local dish left for us was loco moco, both the 'official' version served at Hilo's semi-famous Cafe 100, and the many variations we created or were served by others. Loco moco's origin has been traced to the time when a local footballer known as "Crazy" (or "Loco") asked the proprietors of Hilo's Lincoln Grill for something more filling than the usual budget dish for young men, saimin noodles. Loco moco was the result: a bowl of rice, topped by a hamburger (or other meat), topped by rich brown gravy, with a fried egg sitting on the top. The dish spread from Hilo to the rest of the islands, and now, watch out, it may be headed for your dining room.

Ingredients

rice
meat—hamburger, bacon, ham, Portuguese sausage, teriyaki chicken or beef,
    fish (such as mahimahi), kalua pork, shrimp, oysters, or, of course, Spam
thick brown gravy
fried egg

Preparation

• Cooked rice in the big bowl. Meat on the rice. Gravy on the meat. Egg on the gravy, smile on the face.

This fine technical drawing comes from the Educational Media Center at Kapi`olani Community College. Honolulu, Hawaii. Their helpful website is at http://naio.kcc.hawaii.edu/tours/grinds/default.html

MEAL IN A RICE COOKER

Don McDonald shared with us this ingenious way to prepare an entire meal in an ordinary rice cooker. You can do this with almost any frozen vegetable and a lot of fresh ones as well, so use your favorites.

Ingredients
1   cup white rice
2½ cups chicken stock or canned chicken bouillon
1   bay leaf
4   ounces frozen boneless skinless chicken breast
     Lots of vegetables, fresh or frozen such as:
         broccoli, cauliflower, asparagus

Preparation
• Put the rice in the rice cooker
• Add the liquid and bay leaf
• Cut the chicken breast into 3 or 4 pieces
• Add the chicken and vegetables.
• Put the top on and start the rice cooker.
• When it shuts off, everything will be done to perfection, and dinner is served.

Serves 1

MEAT STRAPPED TO THE ENGINE OF YOUR CAR AND COOKED AS YOU DRIVE ALONG

It is possible, believe it or not, to strap various foodstuffs to the engine of your car and cook them with engine heat as you drive along the highway. In fact it is not only possible, it can be a convenient, economical, and decidedly unusual way to take your meals while on a trip. The basic technique, for all foods, is to wrap the raw food in three layers of heavy-duty foil, being sure the wrap is airtight—both to keep food juices in and engine juices out. The packet of food is placed next to or wired onto the exhaust manifold of the car: those pipes coming out of the main engine eventually leading to the muffler. But every engine is different. Indeed, on V-8 engines, the food packet is best fastened right on the engine block, between the cylinders.

Then drive. At normal highway speeds, the cooking time will vary from half an hour for hot dogs up to nearly 5 hours for chicken or roast beef.

The main drawback to this technique is the danger of being arrested and thrown into the local Home for the Odd. ("Having trouble, there, bud?" "No, officer, I'm strapping a chicken to my engine." "May I ask *why* you think you're strapping a chicken to your engine?" "Yes, sir, because we're all out of beef stew.")

The chart on the next page tells you how to do it. Testing and improvising as necessary, based on your car and driving habits. Cooking mileage may vary.

Food item	Approximate Cooking Mileage	Special Instructions
Hot dogs	25	Wrap them side by side
Hamburgers	40 to 50 for rare 50 to 60 for medium 60 to 70 for well done	Wrap side by side. Add barbecue sauce and onions if you wish
Chicken	250 to 300 (appx. 5 hours)	Use young broilers or fryers. Cook only half on each side of engine. Splay legs and wings out, to avoid overcooking
Roast beef	150 to 200 (appx. 4½ hours)	Should weigh 3 pounds or less. Turn over at halfway point.
Beef Stew	150 to 200 (appx. 3 hours)	Cut beef into 1-inch cubes. Add drained can of mushrooms, ½ package dry onion soup mix, barbecue sauce, 1 tbsp. butter, parboiled carrots and potatoes (done before you leave; 10 minutes for carrots, 5 for potatoes).
Salmon *Salmon recipe is from Holly Ocasio Rizzo, staff writer, San Francisco Chronicle, as published in the paper on June 6, 2001*	40 to 50	Smear foil with olive oil. Cut fresh dill onto oil. Grind pepper onto foil. Place salmon on foil, top with more dill, pepper, and salt. Drive about 40 miles. If fish is not flaky, keep on driving, 5 or more miles.

MESS OF POTTAGE À LA ESAU

Esau came from the field and he was faint. And Esau said to Jacob, Feed me, I pray thee, with that...pottage; for I am faint.... And Jacob said, Sell me this day thy birthright. And Esau said, Behold, I am at the point to die; and what profit shall this birthright do to me...and he sware unto him; and he sold his birthright unto Jacob. Then Jacob gave Esau...pottage of lentils, and he did eat, and rose up, and went his way."

—*Book of Genesis, 25:29-34*

Gastro-archaeologists (or are they culinary religio-historians?) have been able to reconstruct the identical mess of pottage for which Esau sold his birthright to Jacob. It's really pretty good stuff, but whether or not you think it is good enough to sell your birthright for depends on just how faint you are (and, we suppose, how valuable your birthright happens to be).

Jacob may have just ladled some into Esau's bowl and handed him a spoon, but our family has always eaten the lentils as a bottom layer, topped with a crunchy salad. The contrasts of hot/cold, soft/crunchy and simple/complex make it an unusually interesting dish.

Ingredients for the Lentil Layer

Esau Selling His Birthright (Not a photograph)
Hendrick ter Brugghen, 1626

1   cup lentils
1   tbsp. salt
7   cups water
¾   cup rice (uncooked)
3   medium onions, chopped
¼   cup olive oil

Preparation

• Cover the lentils with water.
• Add salt and cook over medium heat, covered, for 20 minutes.
• Meanwhile,cook the onions slowly, over medium heat, in half the olive oil until they're soft and yellow and beginning to brown.
• Heat the remaining oil in a skillet and add the rice. Stir it over medium heat until it becomes first translucent and then goes white again.
• At that point, add 2 cups of hot water to the rice and when it stops foaming, combine the rice, lentils, and onions in a pot large enough to cook them together. Cook, stirring occasionally, for 20 minutes or until the rice is done and the liquid is absorbed. While it's cooking, make the salad.

Ingredients for the Salad Layer

     Chopped crispy lettuce (iceberg works well here)
     Chopped tomatoes
     Chopped cucumber
     Sliced red radishes
     Kalamata olives
3   tbsp. olive oil
     juice of 1 lemon
     salt and freshly-ground pepper to taste
     Crumbled feta cheese (optional)

- Combine the vegetables.
- Dress them with 3 tablespoons of oil and the juice of ½ a lemon. You may need to add more oil or lemon depending on how much salad you made.
- Add the salt and pepper.

When you're ready to serve
- Spread a layer of lentils on a dinner plate.
- Top it with a layer of salad.
- Sprinkle on the cheese (if you're using it).
- Enjoy, contemplating the current birthright exchange rate.

Serves 4 to 6

MINT FLAVORED MEATLOAF WITH A SURPRISE EGG IN EACH SERVING

So there you are serving up an ordinary-looking meatloaf with a pleasant thick red sauce. Now you are slicing it and serving it. And look! See the expression on your guests' faces when they discover an entire hard boiled egg in their portions. When they recover their composure, they will take a bite and say, "Delicious, and what a charming surprise egg. But there is a little touch of something…" You may then mention that a trace of mint does interesting things to many ground meat dishes, this one included. P.S.: We think this dish is even better cold the next day.

Ingredients

2½ pounds of meatloaf meat (suggested but not crucial proportions: 1 pound beef, 1 pound veal, ½ pound pork)

8 to 10 eggs

salt and pepper

4 mint leaves or ¼ tsp. dried mint leaves

½ cup chopped parsley or parsley flakes

¼ tsp. dried thyme

1 large onion

1 clove garlic

14.5 ounce can Italian tomatoes

butter

Ingredients of the sauce

1 tbsp. instant chicken broth mix

6 ounce can tomato paste

1 tsp. sugar

3-ounce can sliced mushrooms

pinch of basil

pinch of thyme

Preparation of the meatloaf

• Break 2 eggs into a food processor or blender, saving out half the white of one.

• Add 1 tbsp. salt, ½ tsp. pepper, mint, parsley, thyme, onion (chopped in chunks), garlic, 1 Italian tomato, and 3 tbsp juice from the tomato can. Blend it all together. It will green. This is OK; don't worry.

• Take the meat and smoosh it all together well. (Better stil ask your butcher to run the 3 meats through the grinde together; they may even do this at supermarkets.)

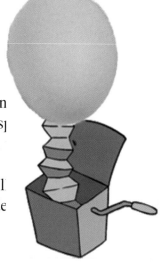

- Mix the blended liquid into the meat thoroughly, with your hands.
- Set the mixture aside for 2 hours.
- Hard boil the remaining eggs, and begin work on the sauce.
- After 2 hours, take half the meat mixture and use it to line a large buttered casserole or shallow baking dish. The shape isn't too important; ideally half the meat should cover the bottom to a depth of about 1 inch.
- Peel the eggs and arrange them symmetrically on the meat: side by side, end to end, or whatever looks pretty. It doesn't matter if they are touching. If they won't fit, cut off the ends. (Of the eggs, not the casserole. This is not the Procrustes Cookbook.)
- Take the remaining half of the meat mixture and pat it gently down on top of the eggs, pushing the eggs down a bit into the bottom half until the eggs are completely covered, and the top of the meatloaf is level.
- Coat the top of the meatloaf with the egg white you saved, and rub it down the sides with your hands as far as you can.
- Put 4 or 5 dabs of butter on top.
- Bake for 15 minutes at 450°.

Preparation of the sauce
- Put in a saucepan: the rest of the Italian tomatoes and their liquid, the chicken broth mix, sugar, basil, thyme, and about ⅔ of the tomato paste (you won't need the rest), plus all the juice from the can of mushrooms.
- Cook over medium heat, covered, for 20 minutes, stirring occasionally.

Putting it all together
- Reduce the heat on the meatloaf to 400°.
- Pour the sauce over the meat, and sprinkle on the mushrooms.
- Bake for 45 minutes.
- Remove from the oven and let stand for 15 minutes before slicing.
- Slice according to where the eggs are. If you think you may forget, you can either mark each egg's location with a stuffed olive, or you can make the sort of map that pirates make to remember where their treasure is buried.

Serves as many people as there are buried eggs.

MINTED BARBECUED FISH WITH AN ABSURD AMOUNT OF HOT RED PEPPER

Without the coconut milk as a tempering agent, this would be the sort of dish that could put your mouth out of commission for a week. So, for goodness sake, don't forget the coconut milk. And don't forget that the coconut milk is *not* the juice from a coconut (at least in this recipe), but rather water plus coconut meat.

Ingredients

½   cup shredded coconut (fresh or dried) Note: This is to make coconut milk. If your supermarket sells canned coconut milk, you can use that instead.

2   pounds of fish (bass, carp, pike will do fine)

1   tbsp. ground hot red pepper. (That's "tablespoon" with a big T, which rhymes with V, which means Very Hot)

10   mint leaves

2   cups water

1   tsp. turmeric

Preparation

• Make the coconut milk by soaking the coconut meat in the water for 30 minutes, then pressing the meat through a sieve back into the water.

• Wash the fish, cut diagonal slash in each side about 1 inch apart, and put it (or them) in a casserole dish.

• Mix all the other ingredients together and pour over the fish.

• Bake at 350° until the fish is done, probably 30 to 35 minutes.

Serves 4 to 6

NINE-LAYER FISH CASSEROLE WITH SAUERKRAUT, BEER, AND GRUYERE CHEESE

When the Committee for the Determination of Unusualness (all two of us) rejected this dish for inclusion in the book, there was a lingering feeling that we might have made a mistake. Fish casserole? No big deal. But wait: 9 layers. Yes, that's a bit unusual. Sauerkraut cooked in beer for five hours? Not your everyday vegetable. A cup of Gruyere? Plus the fact that it really tastes good? OK, then, here it is back in the book. While the original recipe called for carp, it is the case that it will work just fine with striped bass, catfish, cod, grouper, or snapper.

Ingredients
4 pounds sauerkraut
4 garlic cloves
1 tbsp. coarse ground pepper
1½ quarts beer (4 cans)
¼ cup soft bread crumbs
4 fish fillets, 6-8 oz. per person
   flour
2 tbsp. butter or bacon fat
1 cup grated Gruyere cheese
½ pint sour cream

Preparation
• Drain the sauerkraut and cook it mixed with garlic and pepper in the beer for 5 hours over low heat in a covered pot. Drain.
• Dredge the fish in flour and sauté in butter or bacon fat until brown on both sides.
• Butter a 3-quart baking dish, and make a layer of sauerkraut on the bottom, using about one third of it. Then add a layer of cheese, then a layer of fish, finally a layer of sour cream on top. Repeat these four layers one more time, and finish with a third layer of sauerkraut on top.
• Sprinkle with a bit of grated cheese and bread crumbs. Dot with butter and bake at 350° for 30 minutes.

Serves 8

THE ONE-AND-ONLY ORIGINAL FULL DINNER PAIL

You have heard of the full dinner pail from your friendly neighborhood politician—or at least you did back in 1932. Have you ever wondered what a dinner pail was? Well here it is, with a full dinner for four packed inside, along with alternating layers of sand, which you don't have to eat.

Ingredients

4	legs and thighs of chicken	
8	ears corn	butter, softened
4	large potatoes	salt and pepper to taste
1	large pail	flour to dredge chicken in
damp sand		hot fat to brown chicken in
		aluminum foil

Preparation

• Rub the chicken with salt and pepper, and dredge in flour.
• Brown well in the hot fat.
• Refrigerate.
• Shuck the corn, cover with soft butter, salt, and pepper. Wrap each ear tightly in aluminum foil, then wrap the four ears together in a single foil package.
• Scrub the potatoes, dry them, coat the outside of the skins with butter, and wrap tightly in foil.
• Wrap each piece of chicken in foil.
• Put 2 inches of damp sand in a galvanized pail.
• Wrap all four pieces of chicken together in a second piece of foil, and place on the sand.
• Add 2 inches more of moist sand, and do the same with the potatoes (wrapping all four already-individually-wrapped potatoes together).
• Add 2 inches more sand and do the same with the corn bundle.
• Put 2 inches of sand on top of the corn.
• Set the pail into a deep bed of glowing goals, and keep the fire going for 1½ hours.
• Empty (using oven mitts) onto the ground, and divide into four matched portions.

Serves 4

OUDE BALKEN MET VERSPLINTERDE VIKING BIJLEN

A wonderful cookbook which we can mention without fear of competition, because, alas, it has been out print for decades, is the *Artists and Writers Cook Book*. Scores of well-known artists and writers contributed recipes and/or commentaries, one of the most interesting (gastronomically) being the above-named concoction, submitted by the Dutch artist Karel Appel. The name translates as *Old Beams with Splinters of a Viking Axe*. The old beams refers to the odd shape of the finished product, and the splinters are the hot Spanish red peppers, which appear unexpectedly throughout, causing one to lunge desperately for the glasses of cold beer with which this should be served.

Ingredients

1   package active dry yeast
¼   cup warm water
½   cup milk
2   tbsp. shortening
1   tbsp. sugar
½   tsp. salt
1   egg, well beaten
2   cups sifted flour
½   pound lean ground beef
¼   pound lasagna noodles

½   pound diced cooked chicken
1   cup sliced mushrooms
1   medium onion, minced
½   cup candied fruit
1   or more Spanish (hot) red peppers
       or 2 T. hot pepper flakes (the
       kind you sprinkle on pizza)
½   cup grated Parmesan cheese
2   medium tomatoes
     garlic juice
     olive oil

Preparation

• Soften the yeast in ¼ cup warm water.
• Mix together the milk, shortening, sugar and salt.
• Add the yeast and the well-beaten egg.
• Stir in the flour and beat well.
• Cover with a damp cloth and let rise for 1 hour.
• Knead for 10 minutes. Let it rest, covered with a damp cloth. Meanwhile,
• Brown the meat in olive oil.
• Cook the noodles until firm.
• Mix the meat with the chicken, mushrooms, onion, candied fruits, and as much

finely-chopped red pepper as you think you can stand.
- Roll the dough out on a lightly-floured surface to a rectangle ¼ inch thick and as wide as the lasagna noodles are long.
- Cover it with a damp cloth and let rise1 more hour.
- Cover the dough with the meat mixture, and sprinkle lightly with garlic juice.
- Arrange the noodles lengthwise across the width of the rolled dough.
- Sprinkle with grated cheese.
- Roll the whole thing up as you would a jelly roll, so that the noodles are parallel to the resulting log or "old beam."
- Place the beam in your fish poacher (or, failing that, a big enough skillet) and brown on all sides in preheated olive oil.
- Quarter the tomatoes and add after 5 minutes, along with ¼ cup water.
- Cover tightly and cook 15 minutes, turning 4 or 5 times.
- Serve by cutting round slices 3 or 4 inches wide off the beam.

Serves 4 to 6.

PEANUT HAMBURGER BALLS

You have heard of beach balls and eye balls and melon balls and debutante balls, but what about peanut hamburger balls? This fast and simple dish may well become one of your favorites. It is easy to make, and has a most unusual and engaging sort of taste. Much better than a beach ball (at least for supper).

Ingredients

¾   pound. ground chuck
¾   cup crunchy peanut butter
1   medium onion, minced
3   tbsp. chili sauce
1¼   tsp. salt
⅛   tsp. pepper
1   egg, beaten
2   tbsp. butter or margarine
2   8-ounce cans tomato sauce

Preparation

• Mix the meat, peanut butter, minced onion, chili sauce, salt, pepper, and beaten egg together and form into 12 balls.
• Brown in hot fat, pour out the fat, and pour in the tomato sauce.
• Heat 5 minutes and serve.

Serves 2 or 3

PORTERHOUSE STEAK BROILED WHILE ENCASED IN AN INDESTRUCTIBLE ROCK-SALT SHEATH

Set your table with knives, forks, and, at the place of the guest of honor, an ordinary hammer. Bring the steak, encased in its rock salt armor, directly from the oven to the table. It will look like a large steaming white rock. Let said guest of honor figure out what to do. Crusty bread, a green salad, and a hearty red wine are all that are needed for a memorable feast. You don't want to upstage the pièce de résistance.

Ingredients

4 pounds porterhouse or sirloin steak, at least 2½ inches thick.
10 to 20 pounds of rock salt (plain salt will do in a pinch*)
½ pound mushrooms
   freshly-ground pepper
1 hammer
1 pound sweet butter

Preparation

• The steak may either be rolled up and tied or cooked flat, whichever you wish.
• Sprinkle the steak generously with pepper.
• Make a thick sandy paste—not too wet—of the salt and some water.
• Place the steak in a pan and coat the top with a layer of salt about an inch thick.
• Broil close to the flame (salt side up) for 15 to 20 minutes.
• Then turn it over and coat the other side with salt, such that the entire steak is encased.
• Broil for another 10 to 15 minutes, with the other side up.
• Smash the casing away with the hammer, and serve.
• Slosh the steak pieces around in the butter, which has been melted with the sliced raw mushrooms in it.

Serves 4 to 6.

---

* A pinch of salt. Small salt joke.

POT ROAST COOKED IN TEA WITH RUSSIAN DRESSING SAUCE

The tea leaves cover the roast as it cooks in the tea juices, and they impart an offbeat but wholly satisfactory flavor to the meat. In fact, the only thing it lacks when cooked is . . . is . . . well it seems to be ketchup and mayonnaise and brown sugar and lemon juice and onions, which is why this should be served with Russian Dressing Sauce.

Ingredients
4   pounds (approximately) round roast or chuck roast
1   tbsp. shortening
2   tsp. salt
¼   cup tea leaves
4   cups water
8   ounces Russian dressing (ketchup + mayonnaise; bottled thousand island dressing will do)
¼   cup dark brown sugar
¼   cup lemon juice
2   medium onions

Preparation
• Sprinkle salt on the meat.
• Heat the shortening and brown the meat on all sides.
• Pour the tea laves into the boiling water and brew for 5 minutes.
• Pour the tea over the meat, leaves and all.
• Cover and simmer until tender—about 2½ to 3 hours—turning 2 or 3 times.
• Remove meat and skim the fat off the gravy.
• Strain the gravy, saving one cup.
• Mix said cup with Russian dressing, sugar, lemon juice, and grated onions.
• Cook over medium heat, uncovered, until it thickens slightly.
• Serve with the roast.

Serves 6 to 8

PUMPKIN STEW IN A PUMPKIN POT

Every Hallowe'en, Judith M. Roth, home ec teacher extraordinaire, regales her cooking class with this pleasant dish, in which the pumpkin is both a cooking pot, a principal ingredient, and a charming decoration. It provides meat, vegetable and grain, and it is, of course, a one-dish no-pot meal. When you spoon it out, you get a combination of pumpkin and stew. Ms. Roth suggests you save the pumpkin seeds and prepare them according to the advice at the bottom of this page.

Ingredients

1	onion, chopped	1	10-ounce can condensed cream of mushroom soup
2	cloves garlic, minced	½	cup water
2	tbsp. olive oil	2	cups cooked rice
1	pound ground beef	1	can water chestnuts, chopped
1	4-ounce can sliced mushrooms	12	ounces shredded mozzarella cheese
1	tsp. powdered chicken bouillon	1	medium-sized pumpkin, that will fit into your oven

Preparation

• Cut off the top of the pumpkin, and clean out the insides, and rinse.
• If you wish, draw a face on the pumpkin with a black magic marker.
• Preheat the oven to 350°.
• Heat a heavy skillet over medium-high flame.
• Add olive oil and heat 1 minute.
• Add onion and garlic and heat until transparent.
• Add meat and brown.
• Drain off the fat.
• Add mushrooms, chicken bouillon, mushroom soup, water, rice, water chestnuts, and mozzarella cheese. Mix well.
• Place the pumpkin on a foil-covered jelly roll pan.
• Fill the pumpkin, cover, and cook in oven for 1 hour.

Serves 6.

Roasted pumpkin seeds

• To make this tasty bonus, separate the seeds from the pumpkin strings, but do not wash them.
• Toss the seeds with 1 tbsp. vegetable oil per cup of seeds and a little salt if you wish.
• Spread the seeds on a baking sheet and bake at 250° until dry, about 45 minutes. Alternatively, the seeds can be seasoned and toasted in a 350° oven.

ROAST PAPER CLIPS (AND PORK)

All right, so the paper clips are not the main ingredient (the pork is), but we really liked the fact that the recipe that Ellen Crowley sent us was the only one we've ever seen where the ingredients list included "six large paper clips." This is really a basic Chinese roast pork recipe, in which you turn your own probably-non-Chinese oven into a Chinese-style oven, with use of said paper clips. (Note to readers in Beijing: ignore paper clips.)

Ingredients

¼	cup sherry	1	tsp. soy sauce
¼	tsp. black pepper	1	scallion, quartered
⅛	tsp. ground ginger		red food coloring (optional)
	Dash garlic powder		6 strips boneless lean pork, cut from pork
6	tbsp. hoisin sauce		loin or butt (about 2 x 6 inches each)
4	tsp. salt	6	large paper clips (see!)

Preparation

• In an 8 x 12 x 2 baking dish, combine sugar, sherry, pepper, ginger, garlic powder, hoisin sauce, salt, soy sauce, scallion, and, if you are coloring it, enough red dye to tint the mixture a deep red.
• Add pork, cover, and marinate overnight in the refrigerator.
• Place a wire oven rack at the highest place you can fit it in your oven. And put a large foil-covered jelly-roll pan at the lowest place it can go in the oven.
• Unbend the paper clips to make s-shaped hooks, with one curve larger than the other. Push the end of the larger curve into the pork strips about an inch from the end. Then hang the strips, using the smaller curved end of the clip, from that oven rack at the top of the oven.
• Now turn the oven on, set to 425° and start the pork cooking.
• Fifteen minutes later, lower the temperature to 325°, and roast until tender, about an hour and 15 minutes more.
• Remove the pork from the oven. Remove the paper clips and serve them as a side dish with . . . no, wait, we're saving that recipe for our Office Supplies Cookbook.
• Slice the pork strips diagonally into thin strips and arrange on a platter.

Serves 6 for appetizers, 3 or 4 for a main dish

ROAST SUCKLING PIG

There are some famous dishes that everyone knows about, everyone can conjure up a picture of, but almost no one has ever eaten, much less prepared. And a roast suckling pig, complete with an apple in its mouth, is at the top of that particular list. The reason you've never actually seen one, much less tasted one, has nothing to do with its difficulty of preparation. Honestly, it is no harder to make than a big roast turkey. The reason no one ever tries this is because it just *seems* as if it would be impossible to make; that you have to be a certified master chef before they'll even issue you a pig.

We assure you, the hardest part of the whole recipe is getting the pig to begin with. It will almost certainly have to be special-ordered, and may take a month or more to get. A suckling pig will weigh from 10 to 30 pounds, ready to cook. Contrary to what many butchers seem to think, pigs *are* born all year 'round, so pigs of appropriate size should be available any time, although they are more common around Christmas.

Figure about 1 pound of oven-ready weight for each person. If the pig you need is too big for your oven, you can saw it in half, cook one half at a time, and then join the two halves together again before serving. Houdini may have performed this trick in Cincinnati in 1921.

The ingredients for the pig
1   pig (10 to 30 pounds)
     salt

The ingredients of the stuffing
(for a 10-pound pig; use 50% more fo
a 20-pounder and twice as much for
30-pounder)
1   pound pork sausage
3   medium onions
1½ pounds brown rice

Preparation of the pig
• Wash the pig inside and out with wa
   dry.
• Sprinkle the insides with salt.
• Fill the body and neck cavities with stuffing, and close up with skewers.
• Lace the skewers with string so they won't come apart.

(continued next page)

84

- If you had to cut the pig in half to fit it in your oven, seal the cut ends with a double thickness of foil, and tie the foil on with string.
- Take a rock, or a block of wood the size of your apple, and prop open the mouth.
- Prop the ears in an upright position with skewers.
- Cover the ears and the tail with foil.
- Insert a meat thermometer into the thickest part of a leg, making sure it isn't touching a bone.
- Spread melted butter lavishly all over the pig.
- Place in a roasting pan. If any part overlaps, make an extension out of foil to catch drippings.
- Roast at 350° until the thermometer reaches 185°. This will take anywhere from 3 to 5 hours, depending on the size of the pig.
- Baste with melted butter every half hour or so.
- Remove skewers, lacing, and foil.
- Insert apple in mouth (of pig).
- Rejoin two halves if necessary. Just placing them together is enough, but you may sew them together if you wish.
- Cover the scar with a draped parsley wreath.
- Let stand about half an hour before carving.
- Insert cranberries in the eyeholes, and garnish with cranberry necklaces, fresh flowers, and any other decorations that seem appropriate.

To carve
- Cut the legs loose at the joints.
- Slice the meat from the sides, cutting across the grain, and being sure to include some skin (which is especially delicious) with each serving. The bones will be quite soft and cuttable-through. Some people, not all of them bullfighters, think the crisp ears and tail are the best parts.

Preparation of the stuffing
- Brown the sausage and the chopped onions together.
- Cook the rice and add, along with the spices.
- Let cool before using. Makes about 13 cups: enough for a 10-pound pig.

SALMON COOKED IN THE DISHWASHER

W e are grateful to Ellen Crowley in New York for this most intriguing thing to do with your dishwasher while you're washing dishes. That, to us, was the most surprising part: that you can actually cook your main course while you are washing your dishes. The fish is cooked to a moist and tender perfection, without any trace of soap. And the dishes did not taste or smell of fish. Hey, between this recipe and the tip we reported in our *How to Repair Food* book, about drying off lettuce quickly by using the spin cycle of your washing machine, perhaps we are working toward a book on food preparation with household appliances. Let's see: could you use a vacuum cleaner to . . . oh, never mind.

Ingredients
1   piece of salmon (2 to 3 pounds; other comparable fish will work fine)
     A bunch of dill
     Aluminum foil or, better still, a Reynolds Hot Bag (they come in several
       sizes)

Preparation
- Wrap the fish and some dill very tightly in the foil or the
    foil bag.
- Place the wrapped fish on the top rack of the dishwasher.
- Load the rest of the dishwasher as usual (we assume this
    will be with plates, pots, silverware, etc., not lamb chops,
    pot roasts, and a soufflé).
- Add soap. Yes, soap. Run the dishwasher as usual.
- When the dishes are done, remove fish, unwrap,
    discard the dill, and place on a serving platter.
- Chill in the refrigerator for several hours, or over-
    night if you wish.

Serves 4

SHRIMP BOILED IN BEER BOUILLON WITH BEER SAUCE

You've heard of beef bouillon and chicken bouillon and perhaps onion bouillon. Now meet beer bouillon. After tasting it, you may wonder why we suggest wasting it to boil shrimp in. No one said you had to. This dish maybe served to wee children (in case you know one who you think might prefer it to Chicken McNuggets), since the alcoholic content is no more than that of a cauliflower.

Ingredients

2   quarts beer (4 cans)
2   medium onions, chopped
3   tbsp. wine vinegar
6   peppercorns
2   tbsp. salt
1   stalk celery, chopped
3   sprigs parsley
1   tsp. oregano
6   egg yolks
    lemon juice
2   pounds large raw shrimp, peeled and deveined

Preparation

• Mix together the beer, onions, vinegar, peppercorns, salt, celery, parsley, and oregano.
• Bring to a boil, and simmer for 10 minutes.
• Add the shrimp, bring to another boil, and cook at medium heat, covered, for 5 minutes.
• Strain, saving 1½ cups of the bouillon, and, of course, the shrimps.
• Beat the egg yolks gently.
• Add the 1½ cups of beer bouillon.
• Heat in a double boiler, beating with an egg beater as it heats, until it is frothy and a bit thicker.
• Add salt, pepper, a dash of lemon juice.
• Serve alongside the shrimp, which you may have sprinkled with minced parsley or chives.

Serves 4-6

SOUTHERN FRIED CHICKEN (CHINESE STYLE)

That's southern United States, not southern China. If you let a chef of a certain nationality loose on a standard type dish, he or she is more than likely to inject some of the flavor of his or her native land. An Italian chef would probably put oregano in a hot fudge sundae if given half a chance. And so, when a Chinese chef was called on to deal with good ol' southern fried chicken, it came out sort of half-Beijing, half-Alabama. And all delicious.

Ingredients

3	pounds of chicken
3	tbsp. soy sauce
3	tbsp. sherry
1	tsp. sugar
1	tsp. salt
⅛	tsp. MSG
⅛	tsp. pepper
1	tbsp. sesame oil
2	cloves garlic, crushed
1	small slice ginger, minced
2	tbsp. cornstarch
2	tbsp. water
2	eggs, beaten
	peanut oil to fry chicken in

Preparation

• Mix the soy sauce, sherry, sugar, salt, MSG, pepper, sesame oil, crushed garlic, and minced ginger together.

• Cut the chicken in large pieces and marinate in this sauce in the refrigerator for 3 hours.

• Mix the cornstarch and water, and add to the beaten eggs.

• Dip chicken in this egg batter and fry in 2 inches of peanut oil until golden brown.

• Serve with fried rice and/or honey and biscuits.

Serves 4

SPAGHETTI PIE

There is a whole subset of culinary arts devoted to making things look like something they are not. Cakes sculpted to look like baskets of fruit. Mashed potatoes in the shape of Devil's Tower in Wyoming. The ingredients are familiar, but the presentation is not, which some people find off-putting, and others charming. Since we are among those who are charmed, we are pleased to pass along, for the 1,000,001st time,* Judith Roth's creation called Spaghetti Pie. The ingredients are essentially the same as in a lasagna, but the shape is not (unless, of course, you make round lasagnas).

———————

* Ms. Roth was a winner in a Waldbaum's cooking contest, resulting in this recipe (and her picture) appearing on one million calendars.

Ingredients

6 ounces spaghetti (3 cups cooked)
2 tbsp. butter or margarine
2 beaten eggs
⅓ cup grated Parmesan cheese
1 cup cream style cottage cheese or ricotta cheese
1 pound ground beef or bulk pork sausage
1 onion, chopped
1 clove garlic, minced
8 oz. canned tomatoes, cut up
1 6-ounce can tomato paste
1 tsp. sugar
1 tsp. dried oregano
½ cup shredded mozzarella cheese

Preparation

• Cook spaghetti and drain.
• Stir butter or margarine into hot spaghetti.
• Then stir in beaten eggs and Parmesan cheese.
• Form the spaghetti mixture into a crust, in a greased 10" pie plate, and spread with cottage cheese.
• In a skillet, cook meat, onion and garlic until meat is brown and onion is tender.
• Drain off fat.
• Stir in undrained tomatoes, tomato paste, sugar, and oregano.
• Heat well.
• Turn the meat mixture into the spaghetti crust.
• Bake, uncovered for 20 minutes at 350°.
• Sprinkle with mozzarella cheese and bake again until melted, about five minutes.

Serves 6

SPAGHETTI WITH HAM AND EGGS

Sometimes cooks have irrational desires to combine two old favorites and see what emerges. Like corned beef and cabbage pizza. Or roast beef with Yorkshire pudding ravioli. Sadly this often does not work out very well. One happy instance where it does is this curious dish, in which ham and eggs are served in pleasant conjunction with spaghetti.

Ingredients
1	pound spaghetti
2	cups diced ham
¼	cup minced parsley
¾	cup grated Parmesan or Pecorino cheese
1	clove garlic
4	eggs
2	tbsp. olive oil

Preparation
• Cook the spaghetti until firm but tender (*al dente*).
• Crush the garlic and cook in olive oil for 2 minutes.
• Discard the garlic, and fry the ham in the olive oil until it is crisp.
• Beat the eggs a little and add, raw, to the spaghetti, along with the parsley and cheese.
• Pour the spaghetti onto the ham in the saucepan, and mix well.
• Cook over medium heat for 3 minutes, stirring continuously.

Serves 4 to 6

STARGAZEY PIE

We were more than intrigued. We were enchanted, when Jennifer, a New Zealand-based contributor to an education internet group, mentioned her affection for stargazey pie. We had never heard of this traditional dish from Cornwall in the southwest of England, but the more we read, and the more we tasted, the more we liked both the story and the product. It seems that just before Christmas, in the little Cornish town of Mousehole (yes, it's still there!), times were hard. There was little food, and the fishing was terrible. A local fisherman named Tom Bawcock went to sea, and, almost miraculously, returned that night with a huge boatload of sardines. Local women baked the sardines into pies, with their little heads poking through the crust, gazing at the stars (as it were), and a great tradition was born. If you ever find yourself in Mousehole on December 23rd, you will find stargazey pies being served. And if you follow this recipe, you will find a stargazey pie in your very own kitchen, which is a good thing to do. If you can't find fresh sardines (we got ours at an Oriental market), other small (3 or 4 inch) fish will do as well.

Ingredients

2   pastry rounds
6-10 fresh sardines, scaled, cleaned, filleted, heads on and tails removed
2   tbsp. Dijon mustard
2   tbsp. chopped fresh thyme or cilantro
2   tbsp. chopped fresh parsley
2   lemons (finely grated; rind and juice)
1   tsp. salt (kosher preferred)
¾   tsp. freshly ground pepper
12   ounces bacon, chopped, lightly fried
4   hard-boiled eggs, coarsely chopped
Egg wash (1 raw egg mixed with 1 tbsp. water)
6-10 small sprigs fresh parsley for garnish.

Preparation

• Preheat oven to 425°.
• Arrange one pastry round in a shallow pie plate or on a baking sheet.

91

- Butterfly 4 of the sardines.
- Brush cut sides of all sardines with mustard and sprinkle with chopped herbs, grated lemon rind, salt and pepper.
- Arrange the sardines on pastry round or baking sheet symmetrically with filleted side down and heads resting on edge of pastry.
- Fold up and arrange remaining sardines among the butterflied sardines, heads resting on edge of pastry.
- Sprinkle the bacon and eggs over sardines.
- Sprinkle lemon juice over sardines, bacon and eggs.
- Trim about ¼ inch from edge of second round of pastry and place over sardines.
- Brush bottom pastry at edges with egg wash.
- Press top pastry onto bottom pastry between sardines, arranging a pastry edge around each sardine neck so that just the heads peek out.
- Gently press pastry around the bodies of the sardines to make a wavy surface.
- Brush the top crust with remaining egg wash.
- Bake pie for 20 minutes.
- Reduce oven temperature to 350° and bake 15 to 25 more minutes, until top of pie is a golden brown.
- Before serving, tuck a sprig of parsley in each sardine mouth.

Serves 8 to 10

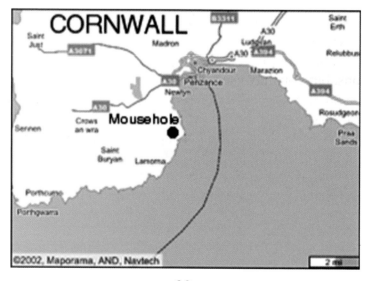

SUKIYAKI CACCIATORE A LA HAYAKAWA

Dr. S. I. Hayakawa was a well-known author and semanticist who became a better-known university president, then a very well known U.S. Senator. He never achieved the same level of fame in the kitchen, perhaps because the following is his only known recipe: a variation on a traditional Japanese dish. He wrote: "The proper name for...my invention...is *o-karibayaki* (o, honorific; kariba, hunting; yaki, cook or broil). I have also heard it referred to as Mongolian sukiyaki. It is said to have originated among Japanese outdoorsmen. The simplified version I am giving here can be made with ingredients that can be found in any supermarket in, say, Topeka, Kansas."

Ingredients

1	pound sirloin or flank steak
1	pound chicken, white meat
1	pound fresh mushrooms
4	bunches green onions
4	large yellow onions

1   tsp. MSG
2   cups soy sauce
1½ cups sweet sherry
2   tbsp. sesame seed
8   eggs
beef suet or
   chicken fat

Preparation

• Slice the steak into thin 3-inch pieces.

• Slice the chicken thin.

• Cut the mushrooms into bite-size pieces.

• Cut the green onions in 2-inch lengths.

• Slice the yellow onions in ¼ inch slices.

• Arrange these raw ingredients on each person's plate.

• Mix all the other ingredients (except the suet or fat) together to make a sauce, and give each person a bowl with half a cup of sauce in it. Give each person another bowl with a raw egg broken into it.

• Ideally there should be one electric frying pan or charcoal hibachi for each four persons, but you may use a skillet on the stove. Melt chicken fat or beef suet in the skillet. Each person should dip raw ingredients into the sauce and then cook it in a corner of the skillet. The very food should be dipped in the raw egg just before eating. The hot food cooks the egg that clings to it, so you are not eating raw eggs.

• Serve with rice and Japanese pickles. If Japanese pickles are hard to find in Kansas, Dr. Hayakawa says that "sliced kosher dills are a good substitute."

Serves 8

TRIPLE POMEGRANATE CHICKEN

Many people have never done anything with a pomegranate other than pass them by in the supermarket. But a pomegranate can add a wealth of subtle and deep flavor to things such as chicken, for instance. So, based on that fine old adage that "anything worth doing is worth overdoing," here's your opportunity to go the whole hog (or, rather, the whole pomegranate), with this interesting recipe calling for pomegranate juice, pomegranate sauce, and pomegranate seed garni.

Ingredients

2	medium pomegranates	1	medium onion
6	large chicken legs and thighs	1	tbsp. tomato paste
¼	tsp. poultry seasoning	1½	cups chicken broth
⅛	tsp. pepper	1	tsp. cinnamon
1	tsp. salt	2	tsp. lemon juice
2	tbsp. salad oil	2	tsp. sugar
2	tbsp. butter or margarine	1½	tsp. cornstarch
	orange slices		parsley

Preparation

- Cut the pomegranates in half, and save a spoonful of seeds for later.
- Squeeze the halves on an orange juicer until you have ¾ cup of juice.
- Rub the chicken with a mixture of salt, pepper, and poultry seasoning.
- Heat the oil and butter together, and brown the chicken well in it.
- Place chicken in a shallow baking dish.
- Drain the pan you browned the chicken in, but save 1 tbsp. of drippings.
- Sauté the onion (chopped fine) in that tablespoon of drippings until soft.
- Add tomato paste, broth, lemon juice, cinnamon, and pomegranate juice.
- Bring to a boil, and simmer uncovered for 10 minutes, stirring once or twice.
- Add the sugar, tasting as you do (you may not want it all).
- Pour the sauce over the chicken, cover, and bake at 350° for 30 minutes.
- Uncover and bake 15 minutes more.
- Place chicken on a heated serving platter.
- In a saucepan, heat the sauce plus the cornstarch dissolved in 1 tbsp. of cold water, until it becomes thick and clear.
- Garnish the chicken with pomegranate seeds, orange slices, and sprigs of parsley.

Serves 6

TRIPLE PORK WITH JUNIPER BERRIES

Juniper berries, as any serious drinker knows, are used to flavor gin. They also do a mean job of flavoring the mixed pork and vast quantities of sauerkraut in this odd dish, not to mention the dry white wine it all cooks in.

Ingredients

Pork I: 1 pound smoked pork loin
Pork II: 8 frankfurters
Pork III: 9 thick bacon slices, browned

1	carrot, sliced	1	sprig parsley
	lard (or butter)	1	sprig thyme
2	medium onions, chopped fine	2	14-ounce cans sauerkraut
1	clove garlic, minced	1	pint dry white wine
10	juniper berries	½	pint water
			salt and pepper to taste

Preparation

• Cut the pork loin into four slices (or chunks).
• Put the chunks into a pot along with the carrot; cover wth salted water. Bring to a boil and simmer for one hour.
• Sauté the onions in the lard until golden.
• Chop one of the slices of bacon. Add to the onions along with the garlic.
• Mix them together. Drain well.
• Wrap in a cheesecloth bag along with the other herbs and spices.
• Drain the sauerkraut very well.
• Put the cheesecloth bag full of spices into a big pot which can go into the oven.
• Put the sauerkraut on top of it.
• Then arrange Porks I, II, and III on top.
• Add the wine and the water.
• Add salt and pepper to taste.
• Cover, bring to a boil. Transfer to the oven.
• Bake in a 350° oven for 1 hour.
• Remove the cheesecloth bag and the meat, discarding the first and saving the second. Stir up the sauerkraut well and divide into four equal portions. Arrange the meat on top in a pleasing pattern.

Note: During the cooking, if it seems to be drying out, add more wine or water, whichever you wish.

Serves 4 to 6

TUR-DUC-HEN

There is a classic dish, apparently invented by the chef to a Middle Eastern sheikh, in which a chicken is stuffed (sometimes with pearls). The chicken is inserted into a duck, which is inserted into a turkey, which is inserted into a sheep, which is inserted into a camel, and the whole thing is cooked in your basic small-room-sized sheikh's oven. Well, thanks to the excellent FM Company of Lake Charles, Louisiana, a comparable experience can be had in your own home, even if that home is in Cleveland, not Riyadh. The FM people stuff a boneless chicken with sausage, crawfish, and/or cornbread, then insert the chicken into a duck, and the duck into a turkey. The finished product, called a Tur-Duc-Hen (or, sometimes, Turducken), can actually be purchased by phone, and we think it is spectacularly worth the cost and effort. Actually the cost is not astonishing, given that one 15-pound boneless Tur-Duc-Hen yields anywhere from 15 to 25 servings. Note: this is the only ready-made product in this entire book. Everything else requires more effort than making a phone call and whipping out a credit card. But then there is no other product on the market, as far as we know, that qualifies for this book: a combination of very unusual, very achievable, and very very good. Buying instructions appear at the bottom of this page.

Ingredients
1 Tur-Duc-Hen

Preparation
Buy. Cook according to package directions, which will require five hours.

Ordering
Available from French Market Foods, 3935 Ryan St., Lake Charles, Louisiana 70605, Website http://www.fmfoods.com/turduchen.htm, Telephone 337-477-9296, Fax: 337-477-9140. Note: We've actually seen these in several upscale markets, and when we asked at one elegant butcher, in Portland, Oregon of all places, the man at Strohecker's said, "Oh, I can make one of those for you."

24-LAYER COGNAC MEAT CAKE

From the outside, this fascinating creation looks sort of like a loaf of bread. And on the outside, it more or less is. But inside there are 24 (approximately) layers of three kinds of meat, all marinated in cognac. Boy, is it impressive looking when you slice it open. Since the basic form of the dish is not unlike a French coute, it is ideally made in something called a coute mold. However a 5 x 9 (or so) meatloaf pan or bread pan will do nicely.

Ingredients

8 slices ham, ⅛ inch thick
8 slices veal, ⅛ inch thick
¼ pound pork sausage
1 pound ground veal
¼ cup cognac or brandy
1 tsp. salt
2 tbsp. milk

1 tsp. garlic salt
1 tsp. onion salt
¼ cup heavy cream
3 egg yolks (hard boiled and pushed through a sieve)
4 eggs
2⅓ cups all-purpose flour
⅔ cup shortening or butter

Preparation

• Cut the ham and veal in 1½ inch wide strips, place in shallow dish, and pour the cognac over them. Marinate for 30 minutes.
• Mix the ground veal, sausage, 2 eggs, 1 tsp. salt, garlic salt, onion salt, and cream together, and set aside.
• Make pastry dough thus: sift flour and salt into a bowl. Add butter (in small pieces) and hard-boiled egg yolks. Mix until crumbly. Add the 2 remaining eggs, and stir with your hands until the mixture is smooth.
• Take ¾ of the dough and roll out on a floured board about ⅜ inch thick. It should be about an inch larger, on all sides, than the bottom plus the sides of your cooking pan.
• Butter the pan, flour it, and drape the dough into it so it hangs over the sides.
• Take ⅛ of the ground meat and pat it into the bottom of the pan. Then arrange a layer of ham. Then one of veal. Then one of ground meat. And so forth, until you have about 24 thin layers, give or take a few. Finish with a ground meat layer on top.
• Spoon in the juices the meat was marinated in.
• Roll out the remaining dough and cut out jolly decorations therefrom: hearts, stars, perhaps someone's initials, and so forth. Fold the overlapping dough over the top and arrange the designs you have cut out on top of the dough.
• Make a small slit in the top, and insert a tiny tube (either make one from foil, or use a macaroni) for the juices and steam to come out of.
• Brush the top with milk and bake at 450º for 10 minutes, then at 350º for an hour and twenty mninutes.
• Let cool, and serve at room temperature, or colder.

Serves 8.

VEGETABLES AND SALADS

AUNT HAZEL'S FUNERAL JELL-O

Aunt Hazel's "job" was to bring Jell-O to the bereaved. Aunt Hazel's niece, Harriet Abell, tells us that at a family reunion in Arkansas, a group of elderly female cousins decided to bring along old family recipes to share. One of the odder ones came from the time when Aunt Hazel made a trip from Missouri to Oklahoma to attend a funeral. This unexpected dish came from that occasion. Thereafter, Aunt Hazel was regularly expected to show up at funerals with her funeral salad in tow. This is a bit surprising in that the ingredients would have been expensive during the depression, but they are things that one can keep on hand, since the Jell-O bringer never knows when her services will be required.

Ingredients

1   small box black cherry Jell-O
1   15-ounce can black cherries; drain and use the juice
     pecans, coarsely chopped
     stuffed olives, sliced

Preparation

• Dissolve Jell-O in 1 cup boiling water
• Add 1 cup of cherry juice (if there isn't enough juice, make up the difference with water).
• Add the cherries and as many pecans and olives as you wish (or, as Aunt Hazel would have said, "as you think suitable").
• Chill and serve.

Serves 4

CARROT & CABBAGE FRITTERS
WITH DOUBLY HOT PEANUT SAUCE

So there we were experimenting with different kinds of vegetable fritters. Many of them were not exactly wonderful. When we got to carrot and cabbage, there seemed to be some promise, but something was missing. In a moment of inspiration, we concluded that the missing flavor—the one that would make it all hang together just right—was peanuts. We tried heated peanut sauce. Good but not quite there. Then we made the peanut sauce spicy hot as well, and here's the successful result.

Ingredients

1	large carrot	2	eggs
	Napa (or regular) cabbage	⅓	cup milk
1	cup flour	¾	cup oil
1½	tsp. baking powder	6	ounces salted dry-roasted peanuts
½	tsp. salt	1	tbsp. peanut oil
1	tsp. chili powder		cayenne pepper (optional)

Preparation

• Shred the carrot and an equal amount (by volume) of cabbage.
• Mix the two together, and dry thoroughly between paper towels until the mixture no longer wets the towels.
• Make fritter mix by sifting together the flour, baking powder, and salt.
• Beat the eggs, mix with milk, and add to flour. Stir until unlumpy.
• Stir in carrot-cabbage mixture.
• Heat the oil and drop the mixture into the oil, so that it makes 4 small fritters, 3 medium-sized fritters, 2 large fritters, or one huge fritter. Your choice.
• Cook until brown on bottom, flip, and brown again.

Preparation of sauce

• Dump 6 ounces of peanuts into a blender or food processor. Add the peanut oil and chili powder, and blend. The sauce should be of thin peanut butter consistency.
• Heat. Taste. If it's not hot enough for you, add a shake or two of cayenne and pour over fritters.

Serves 4

CHILI STRING BEANS IN COCONUT MILK

Note to food historio-geographers: it is clear that the string beans make this a French dish; the chili, a Mexican dish; and the coconut milk, a Samoan dish. (The recipe was told to us, in Swahili, by an old Chinese Jew in a Turkish restaurant in the Bolivian sector of Copenhagen. Or something. Anyway, it tastes good.)

Ingredients
1   large tomato, peeled and chopped coarsly
1   clove garlic
½   cup chopped onions
2   tsp. grated lemon rind
1   tsp. chili powder
4   tbsp. olive oil
1   pound string beans
1   tsp. salt
1   tsp. sugar
1   bay leaf
½   cup unsweetened coconut meat + 1 cup milk OR 1 cup canned coconut milk

Preparation
• In a food processor or blender, combine garlic, tomato, onions, lemon rind, and chili powder together until it is a smooth paste.
• Heat the oil in a heavy skillet, and sauté this paste for 3 minutes, stirring constantly.
• If you aren't using canned coconut milk, add ½ cup boiling water to the flaky coconut meat; let stand 30 minutes, and squeeze the coconut, wrapped in cheesecloth, into the milk.
• Add one cup of this mixture (or your cup of coconut milk) to the fried paste, along with the string beans, sugar, salt, and a bay leaf.
• Bring to a boil, cover, and simmer 20 minutes,
• Since this dish is saucy, you may want to serve it with rice. Very nice.

Serves 4 to 6

CURRIED CELERY AND BANANAS

Celery and bananas both have quite delicate flavors, and when they are eaten together, the combination is even more delicate, but very pleasant. It is important to use a light oil, such as a light virgin olive oil for anything heavier would be overpowering. It is best to prepare the entire dish just before serving.

Ingredients

1   cup hearts of celery
1   cup sliced bananas
     pinch of curry powder
1   tbsp. oil

Preparation

• Cut the celery hearts into pieces roughly the size of banana slices.
• Cut the banana into slices roughly the size of banana slices.
• Sprinkle with curry powder, and toss with the oil.

Serves 4

DEEP DISH CELERY, BACON AND MASHED POTATO PIE

Cooked celery, as we have elsewhere pointed out, is one of the more under rated vegetables in the National Vegetable Survey. It has never made the coveted top ten. Indeed, it has languished for more than 37 years in the bottom ten. Perhaps if more people make dishes like deep dish celery, bacon and mashed potato pie, poor old celery will one day walk in the sun with stalks held high. A fine dish, especially excellent with a pork roast or other piggy entrees. Our recipe testers declared this dish excellent comfort food.

Ingredients

100 linear inches (or one large bunch) of celery stalks
2 cups milk
3½ tbsp. butter
½ tsp. salt
¼ tsp. pepper
¼ tsp. nutmeg
2 tbsp. oil

1 egg, beaten
1 small can evaporated milk
¾ cup breadcrumbs
6 to 8 pieces of bacon, cooked crisp and crumbled
1½ cups mashed potatoes (made however you like them)

Preparation

• Cut the celery into 1-inch pieces (no leaves).
• Boil for 5 minutes in salted water.
• Drain well, and add to a large saucepan with the milk, 1 tbsp. butter, salt, pepper, and nutmeg.
• Simmer until the celery is tender: about 10 more minutes.
• Let cool to room temperature.
• Add the beaten egg to the evaporated milk.
• Stir into the cool celery mixture, then drain, saving the liquid.
• Butter a 2-quart casserole dish and line with the bread crumbs.
• Lay half of the celery on the bottom, topped by a layer of bacon, and then the rest of the celery.
• Pour the celery liquid over the top, and cover with a layer of mashed potatoes.
• Melt 2½ tbsp. butter and add to the oil, and drizzle over the top of the potatoes.
• Bake at 400° until the top is golden brown, about 45 minutes.

Serves 5 or 6

EDDIE'S GRANDMOTHER'S ASPARAGUS SOUFFLÉ

We were delighted to receive this recipe and accompanying story from Eddie Thompson, who identifies himself as "collector of facts, trivia, and bright twinkly things." Eddie's grandmother was a byproduct of the great depression, and "a very thrifty woman. Thrifty may not be the correct word. Stingy may be better. When she turned loose of a dollar, that eagle was really screaming." Because she was reluctant to pay a high price for "store-bought asparagus," her special souffle was only made on very special occasions. When grandma could no longer take care of herself, it fell to Eddie and his pickup truck to move her from the house that had been her home for more than 50 years. She was most reluctant to go. As Eddie tells it, "When I finally got her out to my pickup truck, she had brought an old dishrag, a coat hanger, and an empty tomato can with her. She broke down in tears, grabbed me around the arm, and promised to cook me some of 'that asparagus stuff you like so well if you won't make me go.' I have never seen a recipe like this in print, or anything close. It is tried and true, but I can never make it, or even pass the recipe along, without thinking of that old woman who, without even knowing what she did, taught me so much about hunting, fishing, cooking, loving, and life..." Eddie cautions that "this thing will fall like a cake if you slam the oven door. Be careful. Enjoy."

Ingredients
3   eggs, slightly beaten
2   cups bread crumbs (use seasoned bread crumbs for different effects)
2   cups milk
1   cup grated cheese (your choice)
1   tbsp. melted butter
1   can cut asparagus (fresh will work, but don't tell grandma)

Preparation
• Mix it all up.
• Bake in a pre-heated oven at 350° for 45 minutes.
• If you double the recipe, add some more cooking time.

Serves 4 to 6

FRIED CHEF'S SALAD

First you make a plain old ordinary chef's salad. And then you do what no chef in his or her right mind ever thought of doing: you fry the salad for a few minutes in a sort of sweet and sour sauce, and serve it hot. It is not at all oriental, because of the ingredients, nor is it much of anything else readily describable, except good to eat.

Ingredients

½   cup water
¼   cup vinegar
1   tbsp. sugar
1   tsp. instant minced onion
½   tsp. garlic salt
½   tsp. prepared mustard
    pepper
2   tbsp. oil
1   tbsp. all purpose flour
2   cups cooked ham, cut into thin strips
3   eggs, hardboiled
½   medium head lettuce
½   cup chopped celery
½   cup sliced cucumber
1   cup cheddar cheese cut into thin strips
1   large tomato

Preparation

• Mix together the water, vinegar, sugar, onion, garlic salt, mustard, a dash of pepper, oil, and flour.
• Cook over medium heat, stirring regularly, until it boils.
• Place the ham in the sauce.
• Cut the eggs into slices or wedges and place the eggs on the ham.
• Add the celery, the lettuce, the cucumber, the cheese, and finally the tomato in thin wedges on the top.
• Cover and cook over medium heat for 4 or 5 minutes.
• Serve at once.

Serves 4-6

FRIED SWEET & SOUR CELERY

Cooked celery is not an especially popular dish in most households. Pity. A good introduction to the taste and the interesting texture of cooked celery is this way of making it with a spicy sweet and sour sauce. To retain the soft-yet-crisp aspect, it is best to fry it as quickly as possible on a very hot skillet.

Ingredients
1   pound celery, cut in small pieces
1   tbsp. cornstarch
2   tbsp. water
1   tbsp. soy sauce
4   tbsp. sugar
3   tbsp. vinegar
½   tsp. salt
3   drops Tabasco sauce
2   tbsp. peanut (or other) oil

Preparation
• Mix the cornstarch and water together.
• Mix the soy sauce, sugar, vinegar, salt, and Tabasco together.
• Heat skillet to very hot.
• Heat the oil.
• Add the celery, and fry for 4 minutes, stirring constantly.
• Add the sauce and keep frying, stirring, for 2 minutes longer.
• Add the cornstarch plus water, and fry, stirring, for one minute more. Serve at once.

Serves 4 to 6

LEEK & PEA FLAN

On reflection, the main reason we have included this receipe (besides the fact that it is unusual and tasty) is that it is such fun to say. Try it ten times fast. Leek-and-pea-flan, leek-and-pea-flan. Leek-and-flea-pan. Peek and lee flan. Fleek and lee pan. Whatever.

Ingredients

1   pound leeks, trimmed, sliced and washed
4   ounces fresh or frozen shelled peas
¼   pint fresh milk
5   ounces plain yogurt
    salt and pepper to taste

3   eggs
6   ounces wholewheat flour
4   ounces cheddar cheese, grated
3   ounces butter

Preparation

• Cook the leeks and peas in lightly salted water in a tightly-covered saucepan until tender.
• Drain well.
• Puree together the leeks, peas, milk, and yogurt in a blender or food processor.
• Beat two eggs into the puree and season to taste.
• Lightly beat the remaining egg in a bowl.
• Pour flour and half the cheese in another bowl, and rub in the butter until it resembles fine bread crumbs, then bind together with the remaining egg.
• Roll out the pastry on a lightly floured surface, and then use it to line a 9-inch flan dish. A 9" pie pan will also do.
• Pour in the leek mixture, then sprinkle on the remaining cheese.
• Line a jelly roll pan or cookie pan with foil and put the flan there upon.
• Bake at 375° for 50 to 55 minutes, un-til golden.

Serves 4 to 6

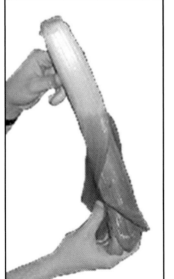

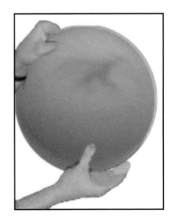

Leek (left) and pea (right). Not to scale.

POTATO PANCAKES WITH FRIED EGGS, AVOCADOS, AND PEANUT SAUCE

In a recent contest held around our house, this odd collection of foodments was voted one of the Five Most Interesting Ecuadorian Recipes of the Year. We have adjusted is slightly, to make it a bit less Ecuadorian (sorry, Ecuadorians), and, we think, a bit more tasty. It can be served for any meal of the day, but we like it for breakfast.

Ingredients of the pancakes

2½	pounds potatoes	½	cup minced onions
¾	tsp. salt	¼	pound cream cheese
¼	tsp. white pepper	8	eggs
6	tbsp. butter	2	avocados

Ingredients of the peanut sauce

2	tbsp. butter	½	tsp. salt
½	cup chopped onions	½	tsp. black pepper
½	cup diced tomatoes	½	cup ground peanuts
2	tbsp. minced green peppers	½	cup water
			chopped green onions (for garnish)

Preparation of the pancakes

• Boil potatoes until tender.
• Drain, peel, and mash, with salt, pepper, 2 tbsp. butter, and the eggs.
• Melt 1 tbsp. butter in a skillet and brown the onions. Stir in the cream cheese, mashing and mixing until it's all uniform. Cool.
• Mold potatoes into 8 pancake-shaped shapes, press ⅛ of the onions and ⅛ of the cream cheese into each pancake, and cover the filling with a bit of potatoes mixture.
• Brown in the remaining butter, and arrange avocado slices on top.

Preparation of the peanut sauce

• Melt the butter in a skillet, and sauté the onions until brown.
• Add everything but the peanuts and water, and cook over low heat for 5 minutes.
• Add peanuts, and slowly stir in the water.
• Simmer 5 minutes, and pour over the pancakes. Garnish with green onions.

Serves 4 or 8, depending on what meal it is, what else there is to eat, etc

RUTABAGA RING WITH BROWN SUGAR AND BACON FAT

People are generally so busy laughing at rutabagas—they were voted the Funniest Vegetable of the Year for six years in a row—that they tend to forget that you can do gastronomically interesting things with them. Like mashing them up with brown sugar and bacon fat and eggs and so forth, as in this pleasant-tasting (but not amusing at all, unless you make happy faces out of beets as decorations) dish.

Ingredients

3	tbsp. all purpose flour
2	tbsp. light brown sugar
2½	tbsp. melted bacon fat
1	cup milk
4	egg yolks
2	cups cooked mashed rutabaga
5	egg whites
	salt and pepper to taste
	parsley

Preparation

• Mix the flour, brown sugar, and melted bacon fat together.
• Stir in milk and cook, stirring frequently, over low heat until thickened and smooth.
• Slowly stir the mixture into the egg yolks.
• Add mashed rutabaga, salt, and pepper.
• Beat the egg whites stiff, stir a quarter of them into the mixture, and gently fold in the rest.
• Pour the mixture into a heavily-buttered 1½ quart ring mold.
• Bake at 375° for 35 minutes.
• Remove from oven and cover with a towel for 5 minutes.
• Unmold onto a heated plate, garnish with parsley, and serve.

Serves 4 if people like it, 8 or more if they don't.

SPINACH WITH OATMEAL-FRIED BANANAS

Here is yet another unexpected, yet unusually good combination of flavors. Even though the spinach and the bananas are not mixed together, they should be eaten together: a little of each in each spoonful. You will inevitably discover, so we might as well tell you, that the bananas are awfully good on their own. To which we can only reply, yes, but the spinach is *good* for you. Eat your spinach, dear.*

Ingredients

1   package frozen spinach
½   cup heavy cream
4   medium bananas
½   cup coarse oatmeal
     olive oil
     lemon slices
     paprika

Preparation

• Make the spinach according to package directions.
• Peel the bananas and cut in half the long way.
• Dip bananas in cream, and roll in oatmeal. Roll the *bananas* in oatmeal, we hasten to add.
• Heat enough olive oil to cover the bottom of a skillet.
• Fry the bananas until golden brown.
• Top spinach with 2 tbsp. of the cream the bananas were dipped in.
• Arrange one split banana on top of each portion of spinach.
• Garnish with lemon slices and paprika.

Serves 4

---

* Homage to a famous *New Yorker* cartoon captioned by E. B. White. Mother says, "Eat your broccoli, dear." Small child replies, "I say it's spinach, and I say the hell with it."

THIRTEEN-LAYER VEGETABLE CASSEROLE
WITH PUMPKIN SEEDS

Even people who don't normally like zucchini (or people who don't normally like mushrooms) (or peas) (or pumpkin seeds) are likely to like this happy blend of flavors. The pumpkin seeds are the salted Mexican kind, usually used as a cocktail snack. Be sure not to add any extra salt, as the pumpkin seeds will have plenty. Likewise, resist the temptation to add additional liquid: it will look pretty dry before cooking. But enough liquids come out of the vegetables to make the casserole just moist enough.

Ingredients

5	medium zucchini
½	pound fresh mushrooms
2	tbsp. butter
1	large can tiny peas*
1	can mushroom soup
1	medium-sized jar salted Mexican pumpkin seeds

Preparation

• Peel and slice the zucchini.

• Slice the mushrooms and sauté in butter for 5 minutes.

• Grease a large casserole, and lay a layer of zucchini slices along the bottom. Then a thin layer of peas. Next a layer of mushrooms. Then spread with some of the mushroom soup (undiluted). Start over with zucchini, and repeat the cycle twice more, so you have 12 layers.

• Cover and bake at 350° for 30- minutes.

• Spread the pumpkin seeds over the top and continue baking for 15 minutes more. Serve very hot.

Serves 4 to 6

---

* Do not substitute a tiny can of large peas

TULIP STUFFED WITH CRABMEAT SALAD

*I*n our neighboring town of Richmond, California, we have yet to see a tulip in bloom. Yet there must have been a time when Richmond was the tulip capital of northern California, for we found this charming recipe in an old edition of the local newspaper, the *Richmond Independent*. We deduce from the newspaper that this dish was made with fresh local tulip blossoms and fresh San Francisco Bay crab. But the salad tastes pretty good with canned crab, and probably would taste pretty good with canned tulips, although we have yet to see that product in the canned flower section of our supermarket.

Ingredients
12	tulip blossoms
1	cup crab meat
2	tbsp. parsley, minced
2	tbsp. capers
2	tbsp. mayonnaise

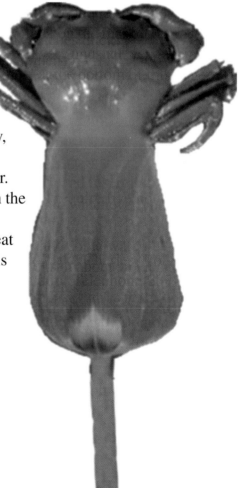

Preparation
- Wash the tulip blossoms in cold water, carefully, and let them stand until they are dry.
- Mix the crab, mayonnaise, and capers together.
- Holding the tulip blossom in your hand, spoon the crab mixture gently into the tulip.
- Garnish with parsley and serve. Yes, you can eat the tulips as well. They are quite tasty in this setting.

Serves 2 or 3

WHITE CASTLE TURKEY DRESSING

Do we need to explain "White Castle?" The world's first hamburger chain? Tiny little hamburgers at relatively tiny little prices. (When we lived in Nashville in the 80s, they were 25¢ each, five for a dollar, and yes, one could and did eat a dollar's worth for lunch.*) The taste is, well, distinctive. Many people like them. Some don't. But if you shred them and make turkey stuffing out of them, nearly everyone will like it. This is White Castle's own trademarked recipe, and we actually had to pay them a one dollar fee for the license to reproduce it here. *Note:* if there are no White Castle restaurants nearby, you can buy the hamburgers, frozen, in supermarkets nationwide.

Ingredients
10   White Castle hamburgers
2   cups celery, diced
4   tsp. ground thyme
4   tsp. ground sage
4   tsp. coarse ground black pepper
¼   cup chicken broth

Preparation
• Remove the pickles from the hamburgers.
• Tear the hamburgers (with buns) to shreds, and put the shreds in a mixing bowl along with celery and seasonings.
• Toss, then add chicken broth.
• Stuff just before roasting, and cook your turkey in the usual manner.

Makes 9 cups, sufficient for a 10-12 pound turkey.

---

* John claims that he remembers when he first discovered them in Florida in 1960, they were five cents each, six for a quarter.

BISCUITS AND CHOCOLATE GRAVY

On the clever website called www.lavaland.com, where people share unusual recipes, a contributor named Sabrina Doster wrote, "I'm a born-n-bred Southerner and had the gall to haul off and marry a Northerner! I was raised on chocolate gravy and biscuits which is my most favorite food of all time. This stuff is the greatest! My husband won't even stay in the house when I make it or eat it though! Oh....and you'll need a bucket....if you like it as much as I do, then you'll eat till you explode!"

Ingredients

Biscuits: 1 or 2 tubes of "whop" biscuits (these are the ones that come in the little tube at the store and you have to "whop" them on the counter to open the tube.) Bake as directed.

3	tbsp.	flour
2	tbsp.	cocoa powder
4	tbsp.	granulated sugar
2	cups of milk	
2	tbsp. butter	
1	tsp. vanilla	

Preparation

• Mix dry ingredients in shallow pan on stovetop until they're completely combined.
• Add milk and stir.
• Cook on medium to medium high heat until it bubbles and thickens.
• Add butter and vanilla. Stir.
• Chunk up biscuits and pour chocolate gravy over the top. Enjoy!

BOXTY

For several centuries*, the people of Ireland (well, some of them, anyway) have prepared a delightful treat called boxty, which might also be called fried potato bread. They ate it plain or buttered as a main dish, a vegetable, or, sprinkled with sugar, for dessert. Sometimes all three at the same meal. If you want to be unbearably traditional about the whole thing, you might dance about the griddle singing "Three pans of boxty, frying all day, What use is boxty without a cup of tea." (Be sure to pronounce "tea" to rhyme with "day." Or "day" to rhyme with "tea," as you wish)

Ingredients
1   cup all purpose flour
1   cup mashed potatoes
1   cup grated raw potatoes
⅓   cup milk
2   tsp. baking powder
2   tsp. salt
2   eggs

Preparation
• Squeeze the raw potatoes in a cloth or towel to get rid of as much potato juice as possible.
• Sift together the flour, baking powder and salt.
• Add the potatoes, the well-beaten eggs, and enough milk to make a medium-thick batter.
• Drop by large spoonsful on a hot buttered griddle or frying pan and cook 4 minutes on each side over medium heat.

Serves 4 to 6

---

* Originally, we wrote, "…the ancient Irish…" But British food scholar Alan Davidson, who wrote those fine words on the cover, pointed out, on reading our manuscript, that the potato did not come to Ireland until the 1560's. Old, perhaps, but surely not, by British standards, ancient.

Irish boxty shop

HAND-MEASURED BISCUITS

Out on the range in Montana, the cowboys rarely carried measuring spoons and measuring cups in their saddlebags, possibly for fear of suffering the laughter of their colleagues ("Hey, Tex, or Monty, or whatever your name is, lemme see your (snicker) Half Teaspoon Unit again" (guffaws).) Still, they liked good food, and some recipes do call for fairly precise measuring. It is remarkable how precise a measuring tool you are carrying around right now. On the end of your arms. The scientific term is "hands." Here is a recipe for delicious tender cowboy-style biscuits, made with nothing but your hands and some heat.

Ingredients

Some flour
Some salt
Some shortening

Some baking powder
Some sugar
Some milk

Preparation

• Cup one hand and take as much flour as it will hold.
• Dip your thumb and four fingers into the baking powder and take out as much as you can.
• Dip your thumb and three fingers into the salt, and do likewise.
• Dip your thumb and two fingers into the sugar, and ditto.
• Dip your index finger into the shortening, and take out as much as you can, up to the first knuckle only.
• Mix the above together (with your hands, of course).
• Add enough milk so the mix holds together. Shape into one, two, three or four biscuits.
• Bake at 450° for 15 minutes (or over the coals of a campfire).
• Serve with butter (and you know how to get it from the butter pot onto the biscuit).

Serves one, two, three, or four. Most likely one.

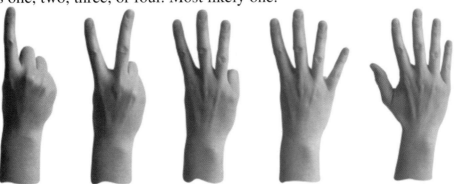

OATMEAL BREAD WITH 3 MILES OF SEAWEED

You know how a vast amount of spinach, when cooked, shrinks incredibly in quantity. You ain't seen nothin' yet. If you can find the seaweed called laver, you will discover that a string of laver about a mile long cooks down to a lump about the size of an egg. That's why you need three miles of it to make enough of these oat cakes for four persons. Laver is extremely fine and glossy. It comes in either green (*Ulva latissima*) or red (*Porphyra laciniata*). You may possibly find it dried in specialty food stores, in which case buy enough to make three egg-sized lumps.

Ingredients
3   miles of laver seaweed
1   cup fine oatmeal
     bacon fat

Preparation
• Wash the seaweed well to remove most of the sand.
• Then boil it and cool it five times to remove *all* of the sand.
• Mix with oatmeal.
• Form into cakes (4 big ones or 8 to 12 small ones) and fry in bacon fat until brown on both sides.
• Serve with bacon.

POPCORN BREAD

Creative people seem to spend a lot of time and good energy reflecting on things one can do with an automatic bread machine, in addition to (here's a clever idea) making traditional breads, or perhaps storing office supplies. Here, courtesy of Alice Tillerson, is a really neat thing to do with said machine: a very tasty bread whose main ingredient is crushed popcorn. The flavor is very very nice, perhaps even better when toasted.

Ingredients

1	package of yeast
¼	tsp. ginger
¼	tsp. sugar
2½	cups 'Better for Bread' flour
2	tsp. gluten
1	tbsp. Butter Buds
	salt
5	cups popped popcorn
1	tbsp. popcorn oil or vegetable oil
1½	cups very warm water

Preparation

• Crush the popcorn, either by hand or in a food processor, until it is reduced in size by half (that is, 2½ cups).

• Add all the ingredients into the pan in the order listed, set darkness control at 11 o'clock. Select "white bread" and push Start.

TUNA NOODLE CASSEROLE BREAD

Alice Tillerson may be Queen of the Bread Machines, but even she has her limitations. While she passed this recipe along to us, it came with the comment that she had never tried it, because it sounded just too weird. We rose to the challenge, and decided that, while unusual, it was really a nice thing to do with your bread machine, sitting there in the appliance garage collecting dust. If there's any left over, it should probably be stored in the refrigerator or freezer.

Ingredients

1	package yeast
¼	tsp. sugar
2¾	cups "Better for Bread" flour
1	tbsp. gluten
½	tsp. salt
6½	ounces white tuna (water pack), well drained
½	cup celery, chopped
2	tbsp. dried minced onion
1	cup chow mein noodles
1	egg
10½	ounces cream of mushroom soup, heated
1	tbsp. oil
1	tbsp. water

Preparation

• Add all the ingredients in the order listed.
• Set darkness control at 12 o'clock.
• Select "white bread" and push "Start."

APPLE-MARS BAR SANDWICH

We found this intriguing recipe on the splendid internet site run by LavaMinds (http://www.gazillionaire.com/food.html), where their listings of Utterly Outrageous Recipes™, found in their books 1 through 6, include lots of stuff far too weird for us, and things like this that fit in just fine. This particular recipe was submitted to LavaMinds by Shereen from Northern Ireland, presumably a place where fruit and candy bar sandwiches are the stuff of legends. Or something.

Ingredients
2   slices of dense, crusty plain bread.
     butter
1   Mars Bar, thinly sliced
1   sweet tart apple (such as a Granny Smith)

Preparation
• Slice the Mars Bar into thin slices.
• Cut the apple into small chunks.
• Butter one side of each slice of bread.
• Heat the Mars Bar in the microwave (check at 15 seconds) or in an oven at 350°, and shkloop onto a slice of the bread.
• Cover with apple chunks, then apply the other slice of bread. Thats all, but for the eating.

ASPARAGUS AVOCADO SOUFFLÉ SANDWICH

Here is a visually and gastronomically attractive four-layer open-face sandwich. The layers, in addition to the toast-bread (is there a word for bread toasted on only one side?), are ham, asparagus, avocado, and a simple soufflé mixture. Etiquette demands that such a sandwich be eaten with a knife and fork. However you have our permission to tell Etiquette what you think of her (him?) and pick this up with your hands.

Ingredients

4	slices of bread
16	spears asparagus, steamed
4	slices ham
2	egg whites, beaten until stiff
⅔	cup mayonnaise
1	medium avocado

Preparation

- Toast the bread on one side only.
- Put a slice of ham and four hot asparagus spears on the untoasted side of each piece.
- Heat under broiler for 1 minute.
- Fold beaten egg whites into the mayonnaise.
- Peel and slice the avocado.
- Put avocado slices atop the asparagus spears.
- Spread mayonnaise and egg mixture over the avocado, covering the sides as much as possible.
- Place under broiler again, until the topping is golden brown: 1 - 2 minutes. Serve at once.

Serves 2 or 4

CHOCOLATE VELVEETA SANDWICH

On the delightful LavaLands internet site,* Brenda Voss reported that she used to take these odd sandwiches to school for lunch every single day. Not only did she survive, but a quarter century later she still thinks they are great.

Ingredients
3   really thick (and we mean a quarter-inch) slices of Velveeta
2   big slices of bread
1   handful of milk chocolate chips

Preparation
• Arrange slices to cover the bread (one slice will probably need to be cut in half or quarters).
• Liberally squoosh the chocolate chips into the Velveeta.
• Top with another slice of bread and press down.
• That's it. Well, you could broil or microwave it briefly, if you wish, but why waste the time.

_____

*http://www.gazillionaire.com/food.html

FRIED PEANUT BUTTER AND JELLY SANDWICH

Once again, those creative folks who hang out at the internet site called LavaLand, have come through with a simple but unexpected sandwich, and a nice story. Thank you to Marlee, who writes, "Some years ago, when our kiddies were all very young, peanut butter and jelly sandwiches had lost their luster and appeal, due in large part to their overexposure (there were 4 kiddies in all). So I quickly came up with a shining new star in the PBJ firmament. Desperation is the mother of invention. This is probably going to be on the menu in Heaven, it's that good!"

Ingredients

    peanut butter (the gorpiest you can find)
    jelly or jam (the goopiest you can find)
    slices of soft white bread
2   eggs
    butter or margarine

Preparation

- Make your usual PB & J, not sparing the peanut butter or the jelly, please
- Set it aside while you crack a couple of eggs into a bowl and beat them.
- Melt some butter or margarine in a frying pan.
- Dredge the sandwich through the beaten egg mixture, letting the excess egg drip off.
- Gently (to prevent splattering) place the sandwich in the sizzling butter and cook it just long enough for the sandwich to brown evenly on both sides.
- Cut in halves or quarters for the little ones, or serve uncut for the big ones.

---

http://www.gazillionaire.com/food.html

INSTANT COFFEE SANDWICH

This is not unlike "A piece of toast and a cuppa coffee, please, and hold the water." You are not, of course, required to eat raw instant coffee, which sounds pretty dreadful. Rather, the coffee powder mixes nicely, on the toast, with the bubbling butter and the hot sugar, and the result is something that is a cross between a sandwich and a pastry.

Ingredients
bread
butter
1 tsp. instant coffee per slice
1 tbsp. sugar per slice

Preparation
• Butter the bread liberally.*
• Sprinkle on the coffee and the sugar.
• Place under the broiler, about 5 or 6 inches from the heat.
• Broil until the butter starts bubbling merrily (Watch it—it takes only about a minute.) and serve immediately.

---

* Alternatively, you can butter it conservatively if those are your politics. The difference, perhaps, is in doing it with the left hand or the right hand.

MARTINI SANDWICHES

Martini-lovers will be glad to learn that said concoction can now be eaten as well as drunk. Now when you are in a fancy restaurant that doesn't serve cocktails, or when your companion starts glaring at you, or nudging you under the table (what are you doing under the table?) to say you've had enough (oh, *that's* what you're doing under the table), you can open your lunch box and extract an innocuous-looking little hors d'oeuvre and sit there innocently nibbling your martini.

Ingredients

1	tbsp. gin
1	tsp. dry vermouth
½	tsp. sugar
1	tbsp. grated onion
¼	tsp. dry mustard
¼	tsp. salt
¼	pound sharp cheddar cheese crackers or toast

How to make it

- Grate the cheddar cheese and mix it well with all the other ingredients.
- If you wish a drier martini, increase the quantity of gin. 2 tbsp., for instance, makes a 6-to-1 martini sandwich.
- Spread on crackers or squares of toast, and place under the broiler until the cheese turns brown and puffs up a bit—just a minute or two.

THE NELSON H. FINKELMAN

We were delighted to receive a communication from Mr. Nelson H. Finkelman, who wrote: "Here is a story about a sandwich that is just what you are looking for. I am eating this sandwich for forty-five years. I discovered it quite by accident. I was making a routine sardine, tomato, and onion on rye one day and I used a knife to spread the sardines on the bread that my wife had used to make a jelly sandwich. The knife had some jelly on it and hence some of the jelly transferred to the sardine sandwich. It was delicious. Since that time, my favorite sandwich is sardines, onion, tomato, and jelly on rye. One problem: I cannot get anybody to make it for me."

We asked Mr. Finkelman what kind of jelly. He replied that it doesn't matter, but we have tried a few, and find that grape or currant seem to work best. Then we asked Mr. Finkelman if we could name his creation "The Finkelman." He replied that he would prefer that we call it "The Nelson H. Finkelman," and so we have.

Ingredients

sardines
sliced onions
sliced tomatoes
rye bread
jelly

Preparation

- Make a sandwich. Make a Nelson H. Finkelman. Eat.

N. H. FINKELMAN

SINCE WE DON'T KNOW WHAT MR. FINKELMAN LOOKS LIKE, WE LEAVE IT TO YOUR IMAGINATION.

PEANUT BUTTER AND ANYTHING BUT JELLY SANDWICH

This isn't a recipe as much as a call for inspiration and innovation, peanut-butter-wise. We have seen many otherwise intelligent and well-meaning people whose entire peanut butter repertoire consists of peanut butter and jelly, and perhaps peanut butter and nothing. What a pity. Sort of like finding someone who eats naked spaghetti one day, and a bowl of meat sauce the next, and never thinks of combining the two. So, as a starting point, consider the happy fact that virtually anything edible—sweet, sour, spicy, bland, you name it—can be combined with peanut butter on a sandwich, and it will be not only edible, but often quite special. Here are just a few possibilities.

Ingredients
bread
peanut butter

One or more of the following:
cream cheese
sliced tomatoes
honey
grated carrots
sliced bananas
sliced bacon
roast beef
small shrimp
slabs of ice cream
marshmallow fluff
cheddar cheese
hot chili beans
sliced apples or pears or peaches

herring
cucumbers
ham
chocolate pudding
prune whip
lox
whole peanuts (not in shell, please)
sliced bermuda onion
crushed pineapple
cashew butter or almond butter
dill pickles
jalapeño peppers
M&Ms

etc., etc., etc.

Preparation
• Oh, come on now.

TUNA AND HONEY ON TOAST

We received a semi-anonymous Email from someone signing herself "Nora," who wrote that she has "a strange food combination that, for some reason, pleases my body. I can't explain why honey with tuna makes any sense, it just tastes good to me and I've been eating it this way for 30 years." Thank you, Nora. We like it, too. And just think—tuna without mayo!

Ingredients
1   hard boiled egg, chopped
1   green onion, chopped
1   stalk celery, chopped
     pinch of salt
     pinch of garlic powder
     sprinkling of paprika
     honey
1   small can tunafish
     rye bread

Preparation
• Chop the egg and vegetables, and stirring up with the tuna and the spices.
• Toast the rye bread and spread with honey.
• Spread the tuna on top of the honey.
• Serve open faced, closed faced, or any other face you wish.

Serves 1 per sandwich.

EGGS AND BREAKFAST ITEMS

BOILED EGGS
STEEPED IN ANISE TEA

There is no way to describe the taste of these peculiar eggs; we can only suggest that you try to find out for yourself. There is, however, a way to describe their appearance. They look just like gigantic unripe olives. If you keep them submerged in the liquid, they will keep for several months in the refrigerator. In that length of time, you may either acquire a taste for them, or find someone willing to take them off your hands.

The ingredients

    eggs (as many as you wish, up to 12)
3   tbsp. Orange Pekoe and Pekoe tea leaves
1   tsp. anise seed
4   tbsp. soy sauce
1   tbsp. salt

How to make it
• Hard boil the eggs.
• Shell them very carefully so the white remains unscarred.
• Pour a quart of boiling water over the tea leaves.
• Let them steep for 5 minutes.
• Strain out the tea leaves, and add the anise, soy sauce, and salt to the brewed tea.
• Carefully insert the shelled eggs and simmer uncovered for 1 hour.
• Put the whole pot, liquid and all, in the refrigerator.
• Eat when chilled. The eggs or you, as it were.

CABBAGE PANCAKES

If you choose to think of these as pancakes that happen to be made from cabbage, then you may serve it as a breakfast dish, along with ham and bacon. If, on the other hand, you regard it as a cabbage side dish that happens to look like a pancake, it is perfectly all right to serve it up with corned beef or some other traditional (or non-traditional) meat.

Ingredients
1	small cabbage
1½	tsp. salt
1	cup flour
3	eggs
7	tbsp. butter
½	cup milk

Preparation
• Shred the cabbage.
• Cook in boiling water for half an hour.
• Change the water, add 1 tsp. salt, and boil for 15 more minutes.
• Drain well, squeezing out all the water you can.*
• Now mix the following in a blender or food processor: the flour (sifted), milk, 2 eggs plus the yolk of the third (you won't need the third white), ½ tsp. salt, and 3 tbsp. butter.
• Blend until very smooth, and combine with the boiled cabbage.
• Melt the remaining butter in a skillet, and drop the batter, by tablespoonfuls, cooking until golden brown on both sides. Makes about 30 to 35 small pancakes.

Serves 5 or 6

---

* In our *How to Repair Food* book, we suggest the notion of putting the shreds in a mesh bag and using the spin cycle of your washing machine.

CHEESE SOUFFLÉ
WITH CONCEALED FLOATING POACHED EGG SURPRISE

This looks like an ordinary, run-of-the-mill, spectacular cheese soufflé. But suspended precisely in the geographical center of each portion is a perfectly-cooked poached egg. How did it get there? Why you put it there, silly. Here's how.

Ingredients

10	eggs		3	tbsp. flour
3	tbsp. butter		1	cup milk
½	pound cheese (any kind you wish)			cayenne pepper

Preparation

- Poach four eggs, being careful not to break the yolks, and drain them thoroughly on paper towels. It doesn't matter if they get cold.
- Melt the butter in the top of a double boiler and stir in the flour.
- Cook one minute and then stir in the milk.
- Cook, stirring constantly, until the mixture is thick and smooth.
- Cut the cheese into very small pieces and add to the mixture.
- Stir until all the cheese is melted.
- Add a dash of cayenne, stir again, and remove the top of the double boiler and set aside to cool.
- Separate the remaining 6 eggs.
- Beat the yolks and stir them into the cooled cheese mixture.
- Beat the whites until they are very stiff.
- Take about a quarter of the whites and mix them thoroughly into the cheese mixture.
- Dribble the cheese mixture onto the remaining whites, and fold it in *very gently*. (Don't worry if all the whites aren't absorbed.)
- Spoon about ⅔rds of this mixture into a buttered and floured soufflé dish.
- Carefully place the four poached eggs in a circle (or, more accurately, a square) on the soufflé mix, and cover with the remaining third of the mixture.
- Place some sort of markers on top of the soufflé to remind you where the eggs lie buried. Perhaps a tiny dot of cheese, a cake fancy, a toothpick, or anything light and visible.
- Bake the soufflé for 18 to 20 minutes in a 350° oven.
- Each serving should be one giant spoonful of soufflé, which will have the poached egg right in the center, much to everyone's surprise, except you (unless you have a very short memory).

Serves 4

CHEESED EGGS
WITH A TOUCH OF BEER

Marie Elena Monaco was kind enough to remind us of a most interesting thing to do with fresh eggs, as modified from the fine book *Recipes from Scotland* by F. Marian McNeill.* The ingredients are not all that unusual (well, except for the beer), but the method of preparation is one not likely to be found away from the Highlands.

Ingredients

2 or 3 ounces of cheddar cheese (mild or sharp, as you prefer) per person
eggs (1 or 2 per person; you know your dining companions better than we do)
    butter
    red pepper
    Worcestershire sauce
1   tbsp. beer for every two eggs
    salt
    hot buttered toast

Preparation

• Slice the cheese thin (do not grate).
• Beat the eggs in a bowl and lightly salt them.
• Put the cheese into a saucepan with very little butter and enough water to moisten.
• When it melts, add a shake or two of red pepper, and a few drops of Worcester-shire sauce.
• Let the cheese cook gently, and add the beer as it cooks.
• When your mixture is quite soft and liquid, add the eggs and stir vigorously over gentle heat until the eggs are well blended in and well cooked.
• Put it on hot buttered toast and serve, being sure to keep the bagpiper's portion warm in the oven until he finishes tootling.

---

* Originally published in Edinburgh in 1946; now Wright Gordon Publishing Ltd., 1999. We hope our book stays in print this long!

CHOCOLATE CHEESE PANCAKES

The delicious story of the marvelous chocolate cheese, available only from the Dairy Store at John's alma mater, Michigan State University, is told on page 46. Once again, fellow State alum Nicole Ballard has picked up the chocolate cheese gauntlet and created yet another intriguing recipe with this product. Let us remind you that chocolate cheese can be ordered by mail, phone, or internet,* and we suggest that your #1 use of it may well be eating it straight from the box. Be that as it may, here is yet another way to introduce chocolate onto your breakfast table.

Ingredients

⅓ to ½ pound chocolate cheese
1½ cups sifted, all purpose flour
3½ tsp. baking powder
1 tsp. salt
1⅓ cup milk
3 tbsp. turbinado (raw) sugar
1 egg

3 tbsp. grape seed oil
¼ cup powdered sugar
1 tbsp. cocoa powder
  butter or margarine
  fruit (strawberries, melon suggest)
     as garnish

Preparation

• Coarse grate chocolate cheese and refrigerate.
• Sift flour, baking powder, and salt together in medium-sized mixing bowl.
• Set aside and combine milk, sugar, egg, and oil.
• Add to flour mixture. Whisk until smooth, then let stand for about 20 minutes.
• Heat pan or pancake griddle until water droplets dance on surface.
• Gently stir chocolate cheese into batter, then drop batter by large spoonfuls onto griddle.
• Cook until top is puffed and full of small bubbles. Turn and cook on other side.
• Combine powdered sugar and cocoa powder. Place pancake on plate, butter top, and dust with sugar mixture. Garnish with fruit, and serve.

Yield: 10 to 12 pancakes

---

* The Michigan State University Dairy Store is at 2100 D. S. Anthony Hall, MSU, East Lansing, Michigan 48824-1224. The website is www.msu.edu/user/dairysto/. The person to talk to is Tamara McArthur-West, phone (517) 355 7713 ext 181. The cost is $4.32 per pound, plus $7 shipping (for each two pounds). Visa and MasterCard accepted.

CHOCOLATE PERCH OMELET

There is a cooking tradition in Mexico, among other places, of using unsweetened chocolate as a cooking ingredient in main dishes. While molé sauce is commonplace on chicken, here is an interesting usage combined with fish and eggs. We are grateful to the wonderfully-named Porfirio Rubinstein for providing us with this recipe.

Ingredients
4   large eggs
1   cup perch (or comparable fish), baked and then chopped into small pieces
⅓   cup unsweetened chocolate, crumbled
1   tsp. dill weed
2   tbsp. dry parsley flakes
2   tbsp. minced onions
      spicy tomato sauce

Preparation
• Beat the eggs lightly, and pour them into a hot greased skillet.
• Sprinkle the fish on top of the eggs, the chocolate on top of the fish, and the other ingredients on top of the chocolate.
• Cook until done, top with tomato sauce, and serve nice and hot.

Serves 2 to 4

EGGS COOKED FOR 12 HOURS IN TURKISH COFFEE AND OIL

You've heard of eggs that are brown on the outside. Now you're hearing about eggs that become brown on the *inside*. Also very tasty. The making of them requires fairly regular attention for the entire 12 hours, so unless you have a professional egg simmerer on your household staff, you will need to be home fairly continuously on the happy day when you decide to make this dish.

Ingredients
4   tbsp. strong Turkish coffee powder
3   tbsp. olive oil
2 to 10 eggs
4   cups water
4   onions

Preparation
• Boil the coffee in the water until the water turns dark brown (about 5 minutes).
• Add the olive oil and boil for another 10 minutes.
• Add the brown outside layers from the onions, and then the eggs.
• Simmer slowly for 12 hours. Add more boiling water as needed—probably every hour or two.
• When the 12 hours are up, plunge the eggs into cold water and refrigerate at least 4 hours.
• When they are good and cold, shell and eat.

EGGS MARINATED IN WHISKEY AND SALT WATER FOR A MONTH

This recipe was designed for duck eggs, but it works almost as well with chicken eggs. Be sure to mark your calendar for the time when the eggs will be done. If you happen to forget about them for, say, a couple of years, it will require the police bomb squad to dispose of them without an incredible olfactory disaster* occurring.

Ingredients
10   eggs (preferably duck; chicken will do)
1   cup salt
1   tbsp. whiskey

Preparation
• Put the eggs in enough water to cover them.
• Add the whiskey and salt. Do not stir.
• Refrigerate for 1 month, give or take a few days.
• Remove and boil in new water for 20 minutes.
• Serve hot or cold.

In centuries past, eggs were immersed in a wide variety of liquids in an attempt to retard spoilage. If you're down to one chicken and you need to make ten omelets, start a month ahead and collect eggs up until your brunch party. Once cooked, you probably won't taste the Jack Daniels.

---

* big stink

FRIED EGG IN TOAST

A cookbook we happened to be browsing through described a dish something like this one as "an old late-night favorite." We have speculated at some length on how a fried egg in toast could become an old late-night favorite. Have David Letterman or Jay Leno dealt with this concept? Alternatively, we picture an urbane, sophisticated couple coming into their swank apartment at two in the morning. She turns to him and says, "Darling, I'm simply famished. Will you please make me a fried egg in toast." Well anyway, you will probably find this a quite satisfactory snack, regardless of the time of day.

Ingredients
    bread
    eggs
    butter
    Aquavit

Preparation
• Stamp a hole in the center of a piece of bread with a cookie cutter. Round is OK, but more interesting shapes are to be encouraged.
• Melt half a tablespoon of butter in a skillet.
• Put the bread in the melted butter.
• Break an egg into the hole, and cook over medium heat. The egg will stick to the bread, so you can turn the whole works over with a spatula, or you can cook it sunnyside up.
• Remove from the heat; remove the egg-&-toast to a warm plate.
• Pour 1 tablespoon of Aquavit into the skillet, return to the fire, heat for a moment or two, set it afire, pour over the egg-&-toast and serve at once.

Serves one at a time

17TH CENTURY GOUT CURE
IN THE FORM OF SWEET AND SOUR EGGS
IN HONEY, WINE, & COGNAC

This recipe was found in a medical textbook published in Germany in the early 1600s. But it is as tasty (and as unusual) today as it was then, although it is not likely to cure the long list of diseases and ailments it was alleged to way back then. On the other hand, if your gout improves from this, let us know; perhaps we can go into business together.

Ingredients

8   eggs
1   cup pancake batter
1½   cups vin rosé
1   tbsp. white wine vinegar
1   tbsp. honey
3   cloves
1   inch stick of cinnamon
¼   tsp. salt
     pinch of cayenne
2   tbsp. Cognac
     clarified butter

Preparation
- Hardboil the eggs, cool them, shell them, and cut in half the long way.
- Mix up the pancake batter (using a prepared mix if you wish).
- Prepare the sauce by mixing together the vin rosé, vinegar, honey, cloves, cinnamon, salt, and cayenne.
- Simmer covered for half an hour, add the cognac, and strain.
- Dip the eggs in the batter and fry them in the butter.
- Serve with sauce in a bowl for spooning over as people see fit. If you don't like the first bite, try again. This stuff grows on you. (But not in the sense of "Doctor, I have boiled eggs growing on me...")

Serves 4

THE OMELET GEORGE SAND GAVE TO VICTOR HUGO

This spectacular creation was presented as a gift by George Sand to Victor Hugo. It is not clear from our historical sources whether she gave him the *recipe* or the actual *omelet*. We rather hope it was the omelet, because we hate to think of Monsieur Hugo having to go to all this trouble; it's enough to make one write *Les Miserables*.

Ingredients of the omelet

8 eggs
salt
1 tbsp. sugar
3 tbsp. heavy cream

1 cup diced candied fruit
½ small can marrons glacés
2 tbsp. curaçao
candied cherries

¼ cup diced angelica
3 tbsp. melted butter
6 macaroons

Eh, Vic, would you like an omelette?   Oui.

Ingredients of the frangipani cream

2 eggs
3 egg yolks
3 tbsp. sugar
2 tbsp. butter

1 cup flour
salt
2 cups milk
3 more macaroons*

*These are the French crunchy almond ones, not the soft coconut ones. If you can't find them, use ¼ cup fine-ground almonds + ½ tsp. almond extract.

Preparation of the omelet

Soak the marrons glacés and candied fruit in the curaçao for at least 2 hours. (You can use this time to write a love letter to Chopin.) Beat the eggs with salt, sugar, and cream. Pour into omelet pan, saucepan, or whatever you make omelets in. Before folding in half, place on it the candied fruit and the marrons glacés. When the omelet it cooked, transfer it to a serving dish, and cover at once with the frangipani cream.

Preparation of the frangipani cream

Mix together the 2 whole eggs and 3 extra yolks with the sugar until the mixture is pale lemon-colored. Add flour and salt, and stir until smooth. Stir in milk, and cook over low heat, stirring constantly until quite thick. Remove from heat, add butter and 3 powdered macaroons, and mix very well

Putting it all together

After you have poured the frangipani cream over the omelet, sprinkle the angelica over the top. Then sprinkle with 6 more powdered macaroons. Then drizzle the melted butter over the top. Heat in a very hot oven (550° is best) until the omelet just begins to brown. Serve at once.

Serves 3 or 4

DESSERTS AND CANDIES

AVOCADO ICE CREAM

One rarely if ever thinks of avocado as a dessert-type flavoring, much less an ice cream flavoring, which is too bad. Get on the ball, California Avocado Board. Until their national advertising campaign breaks, make do with this simple, no-ice-cream-machine-required avocado ice cream.

Ingredients

2   medium avocados
1½   cups heavy cream
⅔   cup confectioners sugar
⅔   tsp. vanilla
1   cup milk
⅔   tsp. salt
2   tbsp. sugar
⅔   tsp. almond extract
1   tsp. lemon juice

Preparation

• Cut the avocados in half, remove the seeds*, scoop out the meat, and mash same until smooth.
• Whip the cream until stiff.
• Fold in sifted confectioners sugar.
• Add vanilla and salt to the milk, stir into the whipped cream.
• Pour in a freezer tray. Put in the freezer.
• When the whipped cream is partially frozen, add granulated sugar, almond extract, and lemon juice to the mashed avocados and blend well.
• Stir the avocado mixture into the partially-frozen cream and freeze well.
• Stir it up again and freeze until firm.

Serves 4 to 6

---

* Simplest way, as reported in our *How to Repair Food* book: wham the blade of a kitchen knife into the center of the seed (or pit, if you prefer), twist the knife, and out it comes.

BABY FOOD PRUNES WITH PEANUT BRITTLE CRUMBS

Just because the manufacturers think that what they are making is food for babies, there is still no reason why you can't treat them as, simply, very smooth, very puréed fruits or vegetables. With this in mind, we hope there will be no embarrassment in acquiring the necessary ingredients. "Birthday present for my grandson," you can say if the grocery checker raises an eyebrow at your junior prunes.

Ingredients
2   large (6 oz.) jars junior prunes
1   cup sweetened whipping cream (or one cup whipping cream to which you add 3 Tbs. sugar when it's nearly whipped)
    dash of lemon juice
½   cup peanut brittle crumbs
    dash of orange flower water (optional—available in Middle Eastern groceries)

Preparation
• Whip the cream and fold the junior prunes into it.
• Add the lemon juice and orange flower water.
• Garnish with peanut brittle crumbs.

Serves 2 or 3 grownups.

P.S. If you really dislike prunes, you can make this with another baby fruit.

BAKED ALASKA FLAMBÉ

Elsewhere, passing off plain old ordinary Baked Alaska as too mundane for this book, we described one with grapefruits inside, served in a grapefruit shell (see page 150). Another out of the ordinary Baked Alaska is one that is brought flaming to the table—a difficult feat because of the ice cream content. Here's how to do it.

Ingredients

1	quart ice cream
	1-inch thick sponge cake
⅛	tsp. salt
6	egg whites
¾	cup sugar
	brandy

Preparation

• Preheat oven to 450°.
• Slice the ice cream and arrange it on the sponge cake so that it comes no closer than one inch from any edge.
• Wrap the cake and ice cream in freezer paper, and put it in the freezer. Freeze until very hard. (If you can, turn the freezer temperature way down.)
• Break the eggs as carefully as you can, because you will need some half egg shells later on.
• Beat the whites until foamy.
• Slowly stir in the sugar, about 1/6th at a time, beating after each addition.
• Then beat in the salt.
• Cover a cookie sheet or bread board with heavy wrapping paper. Place the sponge cake + ice cream on it. Cover the ice cream completely with the meringue you have just made, making sure that no ice cream shows through.
• Take 6 or 8 half eggshells and push them down into the meringue at regular intervals.
• Put the Alaska in the very hot oven until the meringue is brown—no more than four or five minutes.
• Heat the brandy until it is very hot, but not boiling. Just before serving, pour the very hot brandy into the eggshells, and set it ablaze. (*Note:* an alternative is not to use the eggshells, and to pour the hot but non-flaming brandy directly onto the meringue. It's spectacular in a darkened room.)

Serves 6 to 8

BEET-CARROT CAKE

Now that carrot cake has gone from an oddity to a common dessert in one generation, creative cooks turn their eyes and cake pans to other vegetables, looking for the next veggie treat. Susan Colledge's eyes landed on a beet, and she has shared with us her recipe for this moist and crumbly beet and carrot cake.

Ingredients

¾	cup vegetable oil	¾	tsp. salt
1½	cups sugar	1	tsp. cinnamon
3	eggs, separated	1	cup grated raw carrots
1	tsp. vanilla extract	1	cup grated cooked beets
2	cups all purpose flour	½	cup chopped walnuts
3	tsp. baking powder		

Preparation

- Beat together the oil, sugar, egg yolks, vanilla, and 3 tbsp. hot water.
- Add remaining ingredients, except egg whites and mix well.
- Fold in stiffly-beaten egg whites and put into greased 9 x 13 pan.
- Bake at 350° for 35-40 minutes, or until a knife inserted in the center comes out clean.
- Cool in pan on a cake rack, and frost in pan.

Cream Cheese Frosting

2   packages (8oz.) cream cheese, at room temperature
½   cup butter, softened
2   cups sifted confectioners' sugar
1   tsp. vanilla

Preparation of frosting

- Cream the cream cheese and butter together.
- Stir in 1/4 of the sugar, then add the vanilla.
- Stir in the rest of the sugar.

Store frosted cake in the refrigerator.

BOILED SUGAR LUMPS INSIDE APRICOTS INSIDE POTATO DUMPLINGS

This takes much care and quite a bit of time, but we think you will agree at the end that it was well worth it. The sugar lumps disappear into the apricots, but the apricots, fortunately, do not disappear into the potato dumplings. On the other hand, the potato dumplings do disappear into your guests. At quite a rapid rate.

Ingredients

1	pound ripe apricots
1	cube of sugar per apricot
3	medium potatoes
1	egg, beaten
salt	

flour
½	tsp. olive oil
4	tbsp. butter
3	ounces bread crumbs
3	ounces grated nuts
4	tbsp. sugar

Preparation

• Remove the apricot stones and replace each with a cube of sugar.
• Boil potatoes until very soft, and then peel them.
• Push them through a sieve, add the beaten egg, a dash of salt and the olive oil. Mix well.
• Add enough flour to make the dough elastic, so it can be rolled out easily.
• Roll the dough out about ⅛ inch thick, and cut into 3-inch squares.
• Wrap each apricot in a square of dough, and seal the seams together.
• Boil a large pot of water, and gently lower the apricot balls into same. Let them boil until they float to the surface (which should take about 15 minutes).
• Meanwhile, melt 2 tsp. butter in a pan, add the bread crumbs, nuts, and 2 tbsp. sugar, and stir until the mixture becomes dark yellow.
• Roll the cooked dumplings in this mixture, pour on the remaining butter (melted), and sprinkle on the remaining sugar.

Serves 4 to 6, depending on the size of the apricots (and the size of the diners)

CAKE EN BROCHETTE WITH THE CRUST INSIDE AND THE MIDDLE OUTSIDE

Back in the old days, before the invention of the built-in oven, cakes were made on large skewers in front of the fireplace. The dough was dribbled onto the skewer as it turned (or, rather, *was* turned. ("What's your line? "Oh, I'm a professional skewer-turner and batter-dribbler.")). Thus it is cooked from the inside out. Here is how to do the same in your nice modern kitchen.

Ingredients
½   cup butter
5   egg yolks, slightly beaten
¾   tsp. salt
2   cups cake flour
2   tsp. baking powder
1   cup sugar
¾   cup milk
½   cup crushed walnuts

Preparation
• Mix together the butter, egg yolks (slightly beaten), and walnuts.
• Sift the flour, baking powder, sugar, and salt together and add about half to the butter and egg mixture.
• Add half the milk, stir well for 3 minutes, and add the rest of the milk, followed by the rest of the flour mixture. Beat for 1 more minute.
• Put a very small amount on a greased skewer or brochette, turning (automatically, we hope, but by hand if you have patience, children, or dedicated friends), over a fire, coals, or a barbecue unit.
• Keep the skewer turning constantly, and keep adding the batter *v e r y s l o w l y* —at the rate of 1 or 2 spoonfuls every 5 to 10 minutes. You can add it faster as the cake gets larger. It may take 2 or 3 hours to get a large cake—say 7 inches in diameter.
• When the cake has grown as large as you wish (or have time for), slide it off the skewer and serve.

CHOCOLATE BAKED ALASKA WITH AND IN GRAPEFRUITS

Baked Alaska could be considered sufficiently unusual on its own to warrant inclusion in this collection. Most people can count the number of times they've had it on the fingers of, well, one or two fingers. But we have decided against including it, because we have two even *more* unusual ways to make Baked Alaska: this one, and the flaming variation on page 146. So if you serve Baked Alaska so often around your house that everyone has grown tired of it, now you have two variations to perk up their taste buds.

Ingredients
2   grapefruits
1   pint chocolate ice cream
3   egg whites
¼   tsp. cream of tartar
6   tbsp. sugar

Preparation
• Cut the grapefruits in half and remove the insides, being careful to preserve 16 half-segments and leaving the peel intact..
• Place four segments into each half. Fill to within ¼ inch of the top with very hard chocolate ice cream. Return these to the freezer.
• Beat the egg whites with the cream of tartar until stiff.
• Slowly beat in the sugar until the mixture is very stiff and also shiny or glossy.
• Spread this meringue over the ice cream, drooping it slightly over onto the grapefruit, so that no ice cream is visible.
• Place in a 450° oven until the meringue turns brown: only a couple of minutes at most.
• Serve at once.

Serves 4

CHOCOLATE CHIP PUMPKIN CHEESECAKE

When we put out the word, on the internet, that we were looking for unusual recipes, one of the first responses came from David and Penny, who wrote us that they are not huge cheesecake fans, but they happily make an exception for this one.

Ingredients

1 cup (about 30 wafers) vanilla wafer crumbs

¼ cup Hershey's cocoa

¼ cup powdered sugar

¼ cup (½ stick) butter or margarine, melted

3 packages (8 ounces each) cream cheese, softened

1 cup granulated sugar

3 tablespoons all-purpose flour

1 teaspoon pumpkin pie spice

1 cup canned pumpkin

4 eggs

1 cup semi-sweet chocolate mini chocolate chips

Preparation

• Heat oven to 350º.

• In medium bowl, stir together crumbs, cocoa and powdered sugar; stir in butter.

• Press mixture onto bottom and half an inch up the side of a 9" springform pan.

• Bake 8 minutes. Remove from oven; cool slightly.

• Increase oven temperature to 400º.

• In a small bowl, combine granulated sugar, flour and pumpkin pie spice.

• In large mixing bowl, beat cream cheese, add the sugar, flour and spice mix.

• Add pumpkin and eggs; beat until well blended.

• Stir in small chocolate chips.

• Pour batter into prepared crust.

• Bake 10 minutes.

• Reduce oven temperature to 250º; continue baking 50 minutes, or until center is somewhat firm (it'll firm up the rest of the way in the fridge).

• Remove from oven to wire rack.

• With knife, loosen cake from side of pan.

• Cool completely; remove side of pan.

• Cover with plastic wrap and refrigerate before serving (overnight is best).

Makes 10 to 12 servings.

CHOCOLATE FIG ICE CREAM

There is a feeling about chocolate, very likely perpetuated by the Chocolate Purists League: never mess around with chocolate. Oh, to be sure, we occasionally add nuts or marshmallows to chocolatey things, but other combinations are looked at with concern if not outright disfavor. This is unfortunate, since a lot of other flavors, some of which most people never think of, are quite compatible with chocolate. Case in point: figs. Even people who don't like figs by themselves (or figs in crowds at Times Square on New Year's Eve, for that matter*) will (probably) like chocolate fig ice cream. The two just somehow go together. About as well as, as, well as sardines and jelly (see page 128).

Ingredients

1⅛	cups minced fresh figs
⅛	cup apple cider
¾	cup sugar
1	cup grated bittersweet chocolate
⅔	cup whipping cream
1	tsp. vanilla extract
¼	tsp. salt

Preparation

• Soak the figs in the cider for 2 hours.
• Push figs through a sieve.
• Mix the sugar and chocolate together and heat over medium heat until it becomes syrupy.
• Cool to room temperature.
• Whip the cream and add to the syrup, along with the vanilla and salt.
• Add figs and stir well.
• Pour into freezer trays.
• Freeze until mushy.
• Beat well, then freeze until frozen.

Serves 4

---

* You may wonder if figs go to Times Square to welcome in the New Year. So do we.

CHOCOLATE MOUSSE BAKLAVA

Nicole Ballard writes to us that "The idea behind the contest was to develop a recipe for romance. First prize was a trip to New York to meet Fabio. I had zero interest in meeting Fabio; I wanted to meet John Burke and be on *Personal FX: the Collectibles Show*. Well, at least I was one of the second place winners (a $300 set of dessert dishes, thank you very much). The sponsor of the contest was a brand of margarine that has so much water in it, the end result is rather soggy baklava, hence my recommendation for using good old-fashioned butter instead. I think Fabio would like it better this way, too."

Ingredients for Mousse

4	ounces cream cheese, softened
2	ounces butter, softened
½	heaping cup Cool Whip
2	tbsp. strawberry liqueur
3	tbsp. powdered sugar
1	tsp pure vanilla extract
2	tbsp. cocoa powder

Ingredients for baklava crust

4	leaves fillo dough
6	ounces butter, melted
1	cup walnut pieces, chopped very fine (best done ahead; Reserve 2 tbsp. for later.)

Also

	whole strawberries for garnish
1	bottle champagne
2	chilled glasses

Ingredients for sauce

½	cup water
½	cup seedless strawberry preserves or jam
2	tsp lemon juice

Mousse Preparation

- In a bowl, combine cream cheese and butter with a fork, mixing until smooth.
- Add remaining ingredients in order given, one at a time, mixing well after each addition.
- Let stand, covered, at room temperature while sauce and crust are prepared, to allow cocoa to absorb moisture.

Sauce Preparation
• In a small sauce pan, combine water, preserves, and lemon juice.
• Bring to a boil then reduce to simmer while crust is prepared.
• Stir occasionally.

Baklava Crust Preparation
• Preheat oven to 400°. (Very important!)
• Follow instructions from box for handling fillo dough. Lay out first sheet.
• Brush half with melted butter, sprinkle with walnuts, and fold short ends together.
• Brush top with butter and sprinkle with walnuts.
• Repeat with remaining sheets, lining up each one over the previous as you go, until eight layers are formed.
• With a sharp knife, cut the crust into four equal pieces.
• Place two on a greased baking sheet.
• With remaining two, carefully cut out the insides about one inch from each edge. Transfer outsides to the tops of the pieces on the baking sheet. Nip off corners.
• Bake crust for 12-15 minutes or until golden brown and crispy.
(Now: • Remove sauce from heat and allow to cool.)
• Remove crust from oven and let cool.

Assembly
• Spoon cooled sauce over crust.
• Sprinkle half the reserved walnuts onto two dessert plates. Place crust on plates.
• Stir mousse, then spoon into crust.
• Sprinkle top with remaining walnuts and garnish with fan-cut strawberries.
• Chill.
• Serve for dessert with champagne and let the evening take its course.

Serves 2

CHOCOLATE PEANUT BUTTER PIZZA

As Mr. Reese learned years ago, chocolate and peanut butter are a splendid combination. What better way to combine them that in this excellent dessert, from the kitchen of Bernice Arnett of Marshfield, Missouri. The crust is pleasantly chewy, as any pizza crust should be. We find the end result appealing to adults, children and, if she were given half a chance, undoubtedly to Lucy the Dog.

Ingredients
½   cup shortening
½   cup peanut butter
½   cup packed brown sugar
½   cup white sugar
2   eggs, lightly beaten
½   tsp. vanilla extract
1½ cups all-purpose flour
2   cups miniature marshmallows
1   cup (or 6 ounces) semisweet chocolate chips

Preparation
• Cream together the shortening, peanut butter, and both sugars.
• Beat in eggs and vanilla.
• Stir in the flour and mix well.
• Pat the dough into a greased 12-inch pizza pan.
• Bake at 375° for 12 minutes.
• Sprinkle with marshmallows and chocolate chips.
• Bake again for 4 to 6 minutes, or until lightly browned.

Serves 2 in our house, but 10 to 12 in normal houses.

CHOCOLATE POPCORN BALLS DIPPED IN SNOW

I t was the middle of winter in Chicago when we decided to think of some way to combine two of our favorite things: chocolate and snow. And so we made popcorn balls, plunged them into hot caramel sauce, then into a bowl of powdery snow, and finally into our mouths. We felt that hot caramel coated with icy snow crystals was a superb combination. But sadly, for dessert adventurers in Honolulu, Miami Beach, and points south, it doesn't really work with shaved ice, artificial snow, shredded tissue, or anything else.

Ingredients
½   cup popcorn (unpopped)
⅓   cup maple syrup
1   tsp. butter
⅛   tsp. salt
3   tbsp. sugar
40   caramels
1   ounce unsweetened chocolate
      big bowl of fresh powdery snow

Preparation
• Pop the popcorn (or start with a quart of prepopped store-bought unsalted popcorn.
• Make the popcorn-sticking-together syrup by combining the maple syrup, butter, salt, and sugar, and cooking to 275° on a candy thermometer (hard thread).
• Toss and agitate the popcorn in a big bowl while pouring the syrup into the bowl, so as much popcorn gets as much syrup on it as possible.
• Butter your hands, and quickly make small clusters of popcorn (5 or 6 popped kernels per cluster).
• Now melt the caramels in the top of a double boiler and add the chocolate.
• Put this sauce in a chafing dish over boiling water.
• Supply each participant with a bowl of powdery snow and a fondue fork or a long-handled spoon.
• To eat: take a popcorn cluster, roll it around in the hot caramel sauce, extract, drop it onto the snow, and *immediately* scoop it up and plop it in your month.
• Go "Oooooh."

Serves 4 to 8, depending on what else there is (or was)

CHOCOLATE SAUERKRAUT CAKE

Just don't ask. There are some things that just should not be looked at too closely, and this is one of them. Take our words for it, it is really worth trying. We think you'll like the end result. And we can guarantee that, if you don't tell people what's really in it, you can entertain all and sundry (and/or win a bunch of side bets) over the matter of what the key ingredient actually is. (The only person you won't surprise is Ellen Crowley, who brought this recipe to our attention.)

Ingredients

½   cup butter or margarine
1½ cups granulated sugar
3   eggs, beaten
1   tsp. vanilla
2   cups all-purpose flour
1   tsp. baking powder
1   tsp. baking soda
½   tsp. salt
½   cup unsweetened cocoa powder
½   cup drained, rinsed, and chopped sauerkraut

Preparation

- Preheat oven to 350º.
- Grease and flour a 9 x 13 inch pan.
- Cream together the butter or margarine, and sugar.
- Beat in the eggs, one at a time, and stir in the vanilla.
- Sift together flour, baking powder, baking soda, salt, and cocoa powder. Add to the cream mixture a little at a time, with some of the water, beating after each addition.
- Stir in the sauerkraut.
- Put the batter in the pan and bake until it tests as done, probably 35 to 40 minutes.
- Cool in the pan.
- Frost with the frosting of your choice, chocolate, vanilla, or otherwise.

Serves 12

COCONUT COFFEE PRUNE PIE

Actually this is a prune pie in a coconut and coffee pie crust, but what the heck, it all goes into the same stomach (as John's grandfather used to say, eating his pickled herring on chocolate chip cookies—something we do not recommend). You might well think about other interesting pies you could fit into such a pie crust and/or other interesting pie crusts into which you could drop your prune filling. But *this* combination is a good one, and the three flavors go together nicely. And yes, we *know* we're supposed to be calling those lovely moist tasty yummy prunes "dried plums." Look, we are happy to call ugli fruits "kiwis," and we are even happier to call the Australian Slimehead fish "orange roughy," but we draw the line here.

Ingredients

3½	oz. flaked coconut	¼	cup granulated sugar
1	cup strong coffee	½	cup light brown sugar
1	10 oz. package Lorna Doone cookies	½	tsp. salt
¼	pound butter, melted	1	envelope unflavored gelatin
1	cup chopped prunes	1	cup sour cream
⅓	cup prune juice	½	cup heavy cream, whipped
3	tbsp. grated orange rind	6	prune halves
3	eggs, beaten		

Preparation

- Make the crust by mixing the coconut and coffee, and letting it stand for 45 minutes.
- Drain well and spread the coconut on paper towels to drain even more.
- Crush the cookies (you can use a food processor).
- Combine crumbs, melted butter, and coconut and pat into a 9-inch pie pan.
- Bake at 350° for 10 minutes.

Preparation of filling

- Put the chopped prunes, prune juice, and 2 tbsp. orange rind in a saucepan.
- Add the sugars to the eggs, along with the salt, gelatin, and sour cream, and add it all to the prunes.
- Cook over medium heat until thickened, stirring constantly (about 10 minutes).
- Let cool slightly and pour into a pie shell.
- Chill until firm.
- Before serving, garnish with whipped cream, prune halves, and remaining orange rind.

Serves 6-8

COOKIE-CHIP CHOCOLATES

All right, we're on to you. We know that when you are offered a chocolate chip cookie, you surreptitiously study the plate, and "somehow" manage to select the one (or two) that appear to have the most chocolate chips in them. After all, that's what it's all about, isn't it: an excuse to eat more chocolate in a somehow politically correct way, as contrasted with swilling chocolate chips from the bag when no one is looking.

Well let's put our cards on the table, and let the chips fall where they may. For some people ("My name is John. I am a chocoholic."), the sole purpose of a chocolate chip cookie is to deliver the most possible chocolate chips. Clearly, the proportions are all wrong. Why should we be required to deal with the 90% that is cookie in order to get the 10% that is chocolate.

Here is the solution: instead of chocolate chip cookies, we reverse the proportions, and offer cookie-chip chocolates.

Ingredients

1¼	cup sifted flour	1	egg yolk
½	tsp. baking powder	½	tsp. vanilla
pinch of salt		3	cups chocolate chips
6	tbsp. butter	1	cup chopped nuts
6	tbsp. sugar		(optional)

Preparation

- Sift together flour, baking, powder, and salt.
- Cream together butter and sugar until light and fluffy.
- Beat in egg yolk and vanilla.
- Gradually stir dry ingredients into the creamed mixture. Mix well.
- Wrap dough in plastic wrap and chill several hours (overnight is fine).
- When ready to bake, let dough warm slightly. You now have a choice. Using a cookie press with ¼ inch tube hole, extrude a length of dough onto an ungreased cookie sheet. With the tip of a paring knife, chop off and separate chip-sized pieces of dough. Or you can roll the dough out between plastic wrap to ¼ inch thickness. Cut in ¼ inch strips and thence into chips. Square chips? Why not? (This dough doesn't spread much when it bakes.) Bake at 350⁰ for 8-10 minutes, until the bottoms of your chips are lightly browned. Scrape off onto a cutting board or countertop to cool. Beat off wandering snackers.
- Melt chocolate. Either drop by tablespoon onto waxed paper and lovingly place chips and nuts into each puddle, or combine chips and nuts in a shallow bowl. Pour melted chocolate over them. Quickly drop spoonfuls of mix onto waxed paper to harden.

Makes about two dozen 2" cookies

CRAZY CAKE IN A SKILLET

This sounds as if it could never ever work. But it does, and it turns out so delicious that you will be asked to make it again very soon. Isn't it convenient that you only had to use half of the yellow cake mix. Now you can do it all over again tomorrow with a great deal more confidence, and call it *More Crazy Cake in a Skillet*. Everything is the same, second time around, except the page on the calendar.

Ingredients

½   box yellow cake mix
¼   cup cocoa
½   cup brown sugar
1   cup boiling water
½   cup white sugar
     Whatever the cake mix box says to add, except use only half as much

Preparation

• Mix the cake mix with whatever is called for.
• Pour it into a small (8-inch) heavy skillet.
• Mix together the sugars and cocoa, and sprinkle over the cake batter.
• Pour 1 cup of boiling water over everything.
• Place this dreadful-looking mess into a 350° oven, and cook it until a knife in the center comes out clean; at least half an hour.
• Turn upside-down onto serving plate. (Careful:
  It's lovely and gloppy on the bottom of the pan.
  And now you know why you bake it in a skillet.
  Turning it upside down from an 8" cake pan is
  too much to ask.)
• Serve hot or cold (better hot).

Serves 6-8

DOCTOR PEPPER CAKE

Doctor Pepper was invented in a drug store in Waco, Texas in 1885 In response to our interest call for interesting and unusual recipes, Bill LaCroix came through with this one. He tells us that it simply does not work well with diet soda.

Ingredients

1¼	cups Dr. Pepper	2	eggs
1	cup quick-cooking or regular oats	1⅓	cups all-purpose flour
½	cup shortening	½	tsp. salt
½	cup sugar	1	tsp. baking soda
1	cup brown sugar	½	tsp. nutmeg

Ingredients for the topping

⅓   cup melted butter
½   cup brown sugar
¼   cup light cream (half & half)
1   cup grated coconut (unsweetened or sweetened, as you come to prefer)

Preparation

- Boil the Dr. Pepper and pour it over the oats
- Stir and let stand 15 to 20 minutes.
- Meanwhile, cream shortening, add the sugars gradually and cream well.
- Add eggs, beating until mixture is fluffy.
- Sift flour with salt, soda and nutmeg.
- Add flour mixture to creamed mixture, mixing well.
- Add oatmeal mixture and mix thoroughly.
- Pour into a 9x9x2 inch pan, greased and floured.
- Bake at 375°F for 40 to 45 minutes or until cake tests done.
- Remove from oven.
- Mix topping ingredients together, and spread topping over hot cake.
- Place under the broiler. Broil until bubbly and slightly brown. Keep an eye on it—it only takes a few minutes.
- Serve warm.

DRIBBLED WATERMELON FILLED WITH GIN

This intriguing adult-style picnic-type dessert. "Dribbled" refers to what you do to a basketball, not to what a baby does with, oh, never mind. Better you do it yourself instead of renting a basketball player, since the dribbling must be done ever so gently, and you do not need some seven-footer slam-dunking your watermelon.

Ingredients

1   large watermelon
1   bottle of gin (the size is up to you)

Preparation

• The watermelon should be ripe and very cold. Bounce it gently on the floor from a height of 1 or 2 inches, over and over, until the meat inside starts breaking up into pulp. You will know when this happens because you can feel a difference in the bounce, and you will hear the insides sloshing around. This may require from 20 to 30 minutes of bouncing, so you might want to assemble the whole team to help.

• After the insides start sloshing, cut a 2 or 3 inch plug from the top, and pour in the gin.

• Refrigerate and wait 2 or 3 hours. Then you can either cut a larger hole and ladle out the contents, or, if your group is quite friendly, you can cut a number of smaller holes and insert straws.

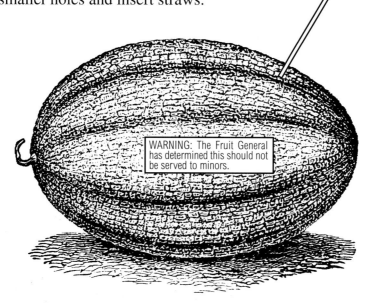

WARNING: The Fruit General has determined this should not be served to minors.

DUMP CAKE

Damned if we do, damned if we don't. The most common response we got when we put out the word that we were looking for unusual recipes, was for some version of dump cake: a cake in which you dump all the ingredients into a pan and, without stirring, bake it. So on one hand, we like the unusual approach. On the other hand, this is not exactly the most rare and special recipe out there. What the heck. Better to put it in and bore a few people than leave it out and deny those few of you who don't already make it the opportunity. The name "dump" refers to the technique of preparation and serving. You simply dump everything into a pan and cook it. Then you scoop it out of the pan and dump it onto a plate. Not only is it incredibly easy to make, but it is adaptable to almost any set of ingredients you happen to find around the house (or dump), with the possible exception of corned beef or old bedroom slippers. Out of cherry pie filling? Use blueberry or apple. No filling at all? Use a can of pitted sour cherries and add a cup of sugar. Do not, under any circumstances, put goose feathers into the batter. That is technically known as "down in the dump."

Ingredients for basic dump cake

2½ cups crushed pineapple (drained)
1   pound can cherry pie filling
1   box yellow or white cake mix
¾   cup chopped pecans or walnuts
½   cup butter or margarine

Ingredients for coconut dump cake

2   cups canned crushed pineapple
       (not drained)
1   cup flaked coconut
1   box yellow or white cake mix
¾   cup chopped nuts
1½ sticks butter or margarine

Ingredients for peach cobbler dump cake

2½ cups canned sliced peaches (not drained)
1   cup flour
¼   pound butter or margarine
¾   cup milk
1   cup sugar

Preparation

• Very lightly grease a 9 x 13 inch cake pan or other ovenproof utensil.
• Dump the fruit in the middle of said pan. Spread it out into a layer. Layer the nuts (if any) on top. Layer the cake mix (or, for the peach one, the flour-sugar-milk mixture) on top. Cut the butter or margarine into small pieces and dump them around on top. Do not stir anything.
• Bake at 350° until done (start testing at 45 minutes; it may take as long as an hour).
• Spoon out and dump on plates.

163

EGGLESS AVOCADO CAKE

This does not necessarily imply that avocados can take the place of eggs in other situations. We give you this friendly warning, lest you are tempted to serve poached avocados on toast for breakfast, or take hard-boiled avocados along on your next picnic. Still, in this interesting cake, avocados do provide the dominant flavoring, and eggs are quite unnecessary.

Ingredients
2   medium avocados
3   tsp. lemon juice
2   cups sugar
3   cups flour
3   tsp. baking soda
1   cup milk
2   tsp. vanilla
2   cups raisins
2   cups chopped nuts
3   tsp. baking powder
0   eggs (a reminder)

Preparation
• Preheat oven to 350º.
• Remove the avocado meat and mash well.
• Add the lemon juice and stir.
• Mix together the sugar, flour, baking soda and baking powder, and sift them twice.
• Combine avocado mixture with flour mixture, mixing well until smooth.
• Stir the vanilla into the milk, and add this to the avocado mixture ¼ cup at a time, stirring well after each addition. Then mix in the nuts and raisins.
• Pour the mixture into a greased and floured 9 x 13 pan (or equivalent*), and bake at 350º until a knife in its middle comes out clean (about 1 to 1¼ hours).

Serves about 8

_____

* That might be, for instance, an 8 x 14, a 6 x 20, a 3 x 40, or even the famous 1 x 120.

EGGPLANT CAKE

This incredible recipe was invented to win a bet. The male author of this work used to believe that eggplant was the awfulest-tasting foodstuff he had ever attempted to eat. The female author did not agree. The male author made a substantial wager with the female author (never mind what) that she could not prepare a dish in which eggplant was the major ingredient, that the male author would not only eat, but actually *enjoy* eating. Amazingly enough, the female author won the bet, and we are happy to share the recipe with the world—a world in which eggplant lovers and eggplant haters may join hands and face the future in harmony.

Ingredients

⅓	cup butter
½	cup brown sugar
2	eggs, beaten
½	cup molasses
	whipped cream
1	large eggplant (see!)
2	cups sifted cake flour
2	tsp. baking powder
1	tsp. salt
	fruit for topping

Preparation

• Cream together the butter, sugar, and eggs, and then stir in the molasses.
• Peel the eggplant, slice into half-inch slices and steam until really soft. Drain well, and puree in blender. Add to the first mixture.
• Sift together the flour, baking powder, and salt. Add to the mixture.
• Stir everything together well, and turn into an 8-inch greased and floured baking pan.
• Bake at 350° until a knife into the center comes out clean—about 35 to 40 minutes.
• Top with berries, berry juice, applesauce, or any other fruit, and, if you wish, with whipped cream.

Serves 6 to 8 former eggplant haters

EIGHT-LAYER APPLE AND PEANUT BRITTLE DESSERT

You can make this dessert with as many layers as you wish. Two is all right, but non-spectacular in appearance, although the taste is fine. Four is nice and pretty impressive looking. Six is awesome; eight is incredible. Ten would probably get you in the Guinness Book of World Dessert Records.

Ingredients
3	medium apples
½	cup sugar
½	cup water
1	cup heavy cream
1	cup crushed peanut brittle
1½	tsp. vanilla

Preparation
• Peel the apples, core them, and cut in quarters. Slice the quarters into ¼ inch thick slices.
• Mix the sugar, water, and ½ tsp. of vanilla together and bring to a boil.
• Add the apples and cook over medium heat until they are tender and transparent. Cool and drain off the liquid.
• Whip the cream, add 1 tsp. vanilla, and fold in the apple slices.
• Arrange a layer of the apple mixture in the bottom of 4 to 6 dessert dishes. Sprinkle liberally with peanut brittle, then another layer of apple, then another layer of peanut brittle, and so on, up to four, six, either, or more layers. Always finish with peanut brittle on the top.
• Refrigerate at least 4 hours before serving.

Serves 4 to 6

EKAC

A few pages back (page 159), we introduced the concept of Cookie Chip Chocolates, as contrasted with the far-less-chocolatey (and thus less wonderful) chocolate chip cookie. Let us now move on to the equally important arena of cakes with chocolate frosting. We've been watching you. We see you slicing those chocolate cakes, so that your piece just "happens" to have about a third more frosting than any other piece. We are aware of what happens to those little pieces of frosting that "fall off" the cake when you're slicing it and serving it to others. And don't even ask about those n ot-too-carefully-emptied bowls in which the frosting was made. The message is clear. For some people, the sole purpose of a cake is to hold up the frosting. And for us, the proportions are all wrong. Why should we be required to deal with a dessert that is about 90% cake and only 10% frosting, when it could be the other way around. Many years ago, John publicly acknowledged all of this, and created the first *ekac*. That's "cake" spelled backwards. The rule is easy. Make a simple frosted cake. But wherever there would 'normally' be cake, put frosting. And wherever there would 'normally' be frosting, put cake. Here's how.

Ingredients

A small cake, white or chocolate, as you wish, home made or store bought.
Lots and lots of chocolate frosting, any recipe, even from a can or mix

Preparation

• Slice the cake quite thin, a quarter inch or less.
• Shape the frosting into two large flat rounds, perhaps 8 or 9 inches across and an inch or more thick.
• For a two-layer ecak, put a layer of cake slices on top of one of the chocolate rounds.
• Put the second chocolate round on top of this layer of cake slices.
• Put another layer of cake slices on the very top, so that all of the surface is covered.
• If you wish, stick vertical slices of cake to the sides of the creation.
• Serve to your happy friends and family.

EVERLASTING BRANDIED PRUNES

Here is the first of two "everlasting" fruit concoctions (see page 190). Like the other, it just seems to get better and better with time, and you can keep adding ingredients as you use them up, so if all goes well, you can bequeath the crock to your grandchildren, and it will go on forever. And yes, we know that the official Prune People want us to call their product a dried plum. We choose to disobey. Come and get us, coppers.

This is really good with vanilla ice cream or plain cake or why not both of them. Some people think it tastes best when you just sneak one out of the jar on your way through the kitchen.

Ingredients
1 pound pitted prunes
3 cups brandy

Preparation
• Put the prunes in a 2-quart jar or jug.
• Pour in enough brandy to cover them—probably about 1 1/2 cups.
• Let sit, uncovered, at room temperature for about a week before eating the first one. The prunes will absorb a lot of brandy over the first 24 hours. Keep them covered by adding more brandy. After that first week, you can start in on them. Whenever the prunes and/or the brandy are low, add more, give a little stir, and wait a week or more before eating.

FLOURLESS CARROT CAKE

If we had done a book like this thirty years ago (and we almost did, but the people at Harcourt Brace got cold feet), we probably would have included carrot cake, since it was quite an unusual concept at the time. Now everybody and her sister knows about carrot cakes, and you can buy packaged slices at the convenience store. And so, as homage to that bygone time when carrot cake was something special, we include a variation on it that's unusual because it has no flour in it other than what is added by the bread crumbs. It is pleasantly spicy and, we think, even better by the third or fourth day.

Ingredients
⅔   cup (firmly packed) shredded carrots
1⅔ cups unblanched almonds
¾   cup fine bread crumbs
½   tsp. cinnamon
¼   tsp. cloves
6   eggs
1¼ cups sugar
1   lemon

Preparation
• Grease an 8-inch springform cake pan and line the bottom with waxed paper.
• Grease the waxed paper, and line the bottom and sides with bread crumbs.
• Grind the almonds (or blend them) and mix with the grated carrots, any bread crumbs remaining, and spices, in a big bowl.
• Grate the lemon rind and squeeze the lemon juice.
• Separate the eggs and beat the yolks together with the lemon rind and lemon juice until thick and creamy.
• Stir into the carrot mixture.
• Beat the egg whites until they are stiff, and fold them into the carrot mixture.
• Spoon the cake batter into the pan and bake at 350º until a knife in the center comes out clean. (Start testing at about 45 minutes.)
• Frost, if you wish, with any compatible-sounding frosting, such as orange, lemon, or spice.

Serves about 8

FRENCH-FRIED ICE CREAM BALLS

What you have here is a sort of puff pastry, very hot and crisp and yummy, completely surrounding a ball of ice cream, and the thermal (as well as the taste) contrasts are quite wonderful. The only problem is that your tongue may become hopelessly confused having something that is at once very hot and very cold placed on it. Consult your medical or psychological advisor for what to do about a confused tongue.

Ingredients

1   quart ice cream (flavor of your choice; we like vanilla or strawberry)
4   tbsp. flour
4   eggs
     peanut oil
½   tbsp. baking powder

Preparation

• Make the ice cream into six balls about 2 to 2½ inches in diameter.
• Turn your freezer down to its coldest position and put the ice cream balls, on waxed paper squares, in the freezer.
• Mix the flour, baking powder and well-beaten eggs together.
• Coat the ice cream balls with this mixture, and return to the freezer until everything is frozen really hard.
• Heat the peanut oil (about 3 inches deep in the fryer) to 365°.
• Roll the frozen balls in the flour and egg mixture again, and fry them in the peanut oil just long enough for the outer pastry layer to puff up. Something between five and ten *seconds* should do it.
•Serve at once.

Serves 6

"Would you like French Fried Ice Cream Balls with that?"

FRIED SPAGHETTI PUDDING

Actually this curious dessert is made even better with vermicelli, the very thin long pasta you'll find on the shelf near the spaghetti. Frying the dry pasta in butter, and then cooking them in water, does most interesting things to the taste. Enough, in fact, to convert it (with the addition of sugar) into a fine dessert.

Ingredients
½   pound vermicelli
1   inch stick cinnamon
½   cup sugar
½   pound butter
2   cups water
    Optional Maraschino cherries and syrup

Preparation
• Melt the butter in a skillet and add the cinnamon.
• Break the pasta into small pieces (2 or 3 inches long) and fry in the butter until light brown.
• Sprinkle on the sugar, add the water.
• Cook, uncovered, over medium heat until all the water is gone.
• Serve hot or cold in little bowls, and if there isn't enough taste for you, stir in some Maraschino cherries and a bit of their syrup.

Serves 4

GRAPEFRUIT CHEESECAKE
WITH GRAPEFRUIT-FLAVORED CRUST

If someone has been complaining—unjustifiably, of course—that your cheese cakes have been too rich lately, make him or her a grapefruit cheesecake with grapefruit-flavored crust. This is by no stretch of the imagination a punishment. It is simply an extremely smooth, lusciously creamy cheesecake that just doesn't taste quite as rich as the usual kinds. For best results, make it the day before and let it set overnight.

Ingredients of cheesecake

¼	tsp. of grapefruit peel.	1	lemon
2	medium grapefruits	8	ounces cream cheese
2	eggs	½	cup large curd cottage cheese
¾	cup sugar		
¼	tsp. salt	½	cup heavy cream
1	tbsp. unflavored gelatin	½	tsp. vanilla

Ingredients of crust

- 2   cups graham cracker crumbs
- ¼   cup sugar
- ½   tsp. cinnamon
- ½   tsp. grated grapefruit peel
- ⅓   cup melted butter
- ⅛   tsp. nutmeg

Preparation of cheesecake

- Grate ¼ tsp. of grapefruit peel.
- Peel the grapefruits and section them, saving any juice that dribbles out as you do.
- Remove all the white membranes, and squeeze the excess juice from those. (There should be about ½ cup of juice.)
- Reserve 8 sections of grapefruit for garnish later, and cut the rest into small pieces.
- Separate one egg, and save the white.
- In the top of a double boiler, mix together the yolk with the entire second egg, sugar, salt, and 2 tbsp. of grapefruit juice.
- Cook, stirring frequently, until smooth and thick.

- Soften the gelatin in 1 tbsp. grapefruit juice, and stir into the thick mixture.
- Remove from heat and let cool to room temperature.*
- Grate ¼ tsp. of lemon peel, and squeeze 1 tbsp. of lemon juice.
- Put these in a blender along with the rest of the grapefruit juice, the cream cheese, and the cottage cheese. Blend until smooth.
- Stir into the grapefruit and egg mixture.
- Pour into the crust and chill at least 8 hours.
- Garnish with reserved crumbs and grapefruit segments.

Preparation of crust
- Mix together crumbs, sugar, cinnamon, nutmeg, grapefruit peel, and butter.
- Save ¼ cup of mixture to garnish the cake, and press the rest into a cake pan with removable bottom (or a 9-inch springform pan). The side crust should be about 1½ inches high.
- Bake at 350° for 10 minutes. Cool before filling with the grapefruit-cheese mixture.

Serves 8 to 10

---

* Why do cookbooks use this phrase? It will probably not cool unless you remove it from the heat.

GREEN CHILE MAPLE PRALINE

One of the joys (and, occasionally, terrors) of the internet is that there something out there for everyone. A newsgroup for lefthanded Jewish dentists. For African scientists working in Sweden. For people interested in Native American recipes, including unusual ones. And from the latter, a group called Native Cooking-L, we were delighted to hear from Sindy Albritton (who is definitely not a left-handed Jewish dentist or an African scientist in Sweden, but instead the owner of Turtle Island Music, purveyor of music and instruments to heal the Earth.*) She has shared with us this recipe for what originally was called "Green Chili Maple Brittle," but we think (John is actually nibbling on some as he types these words) it's a little too crumbly for a brittle, and is perhaps closer to a praline. But whatever you call it, it is a tasty thing to do to nuts. You can simply put it out in a bowl and it will disappear even as you're telling your guests what's in the recipe. Or you can spread softened cream cheese on bland crackers and pat a layer of it onto the cream cheese for a snack that's tidier to eat.

Ingredients

2	green chiles (Anaheims are best) roasted, peeled and seeded	½	tsp. allspice
1	cup maple syrup	½	tsp. salt
1	cup water	½	pound mixed nuts or pumpkin seeds (unsalted)
1	tsp. cider vinegar		

Preparation

• Under the broiler or on a kitchen fork over a gas flame, "roast" your chiles until their skin is blackened.
• Put them in a paper bag to cool.
• Rub off the blackened skin under a gentle stream of cool water.
• Remove stems and seeds and dice them.
• Combine syrup, water, vinegar, allspice and salt together in a frying pan. Bring to a boil, cook on rolling boil for 5 minutes. (Note: boil in a frying pan? Yes. More surface area. Reduces faster.)
• Add diced chiles to maple mixture.
• When the mixture is at the soft ball stage on a candy thermometer, pour in nuts.
• Mix quickly and pour out on a cookie sheet or marble slab.
• When mixture is cold, separate into chunks.

---

*You can find her at www.turtleislandmusic.com

GREEN TOMATO CAKE

Our internet announcement seeking recipes with unusual combinations of ingredients produced this intriguing response from Michael and Melissa Velik, who suggest that this moist spicy cake is a fine way to use up extra green tomatoes before the first frost hits. And if you live outside of the frost belt, you have our permission to make this anyway.

Ingredients

½	cup	butter		
2	cups	granulated sugar		
2		eggs		
2	cups	all-purpose flour		
½	cup	raisins		
1	tsp.	ground cinnamon		

1   tsp. ground nutmeg
1   tsp. baking soda
¼   tsp. salt
½   cup chopped walnuts
4   cups green tomatoes, chopped
1   tbsp. salt

Preparation

• Wash, peel and dice green tomatoes.
• Sprinkle with 1 tbsp. salt.
• Let stand 10 minutes.
• Place in a colander and rinse with cold water and drain.
• Preheat oven to 350º.
• Grease and flour a 9x13 inch pan.
• Cream butter and sugar.
• Add eggs and beat until creamy.
• Sift together flour, raisins, cinnamon, nutmeg, baking soda, and salt.
• Add raisins and nuts to dry mixture; add to creamed mixture. (Dough will be very stiff.)
• Add drained tomatoes and mix well.
• Pour into a prepared 9 x 13 inch pan.
• Bake at 350º for 40 to 45 minutes, or until toothpick inserted into cake comes out clean.
• Sprinkle with confectioners sugar or frost with your favorite caramel or cream cheese frosting.

18 to 20 servings

HOT ORANGE-LEMON-GRAPEFRUIT PIE

If only we had figured out how to include some tangerines, kumquats, and kiwis in this pie, we might have won some sort of award from the Citrus Association. As it is, we think three is plenty; in fact, just right. You may prefer to serve this pie cold, but it is undeniably more interesting hot. (*Note:* We were surprised at the difficulty we had in finding minute tapioca in our neighborhood. If it cannot be found, cornstarch will do.)

Ingredients

4   navel oranges
1   large grapefruit
1   lemon
3   tbsp. minute tapioca
1   cup sugar
1   9-inch pie crust (unbaked)
    Optional toasted almonds and almond syrup

Preparation

• Peel the grapefruit and cut into small pieces (not segments).
• Peel the oranges and separate the sections.
• Grate the peel and then squeeze the juice from the lemon (save the juice).
• Mix everything, including the lemon juice, together, and pour into an unbaked pie crust.
• Cook for 450° for 15 minutes, and then at 400° for 20 minutes.
• Top, if you wish, with toasted almond slivers and/or almond syrup.

Serves about 6.

JELL-O™ POPCORN HEARTS

For most people, the only thing to do with Jell-O powder is—as you might guess—make Jell-O. But Judith Roth's students at Islip High School, get to make these delights with Jell-O powder, especially around Valentine's day. Of course you could use other colors of Jell-O and indeed other shapes, for other occasions: green shamrocks for St. Patrick's day, yellow lemons for the dealer who sold you that 1991 Plymouth Laser, and so on.

Ingredients
10	ounce bag of marshmallows
¼	cup butter
3	tbsp. red Jell-O powder
8	cups popped popcorn

Preparation
- Melt marshmallows with butter in the top of a double boiler, or in a large Pyrex bowl in the microwave for 2 to 3 minutes.
- Add Jell-O powder and mix well.
- Stir in the popcorn.
- Spoon onto waxed paper.
- Use pieces of waxed paper to shape the popcorn into hearts, or whatever.

Makes one huge heart, 32 tiny hearts, or anything in between

Note: The "™" next to the word Jell-O means that we know it is a trademark of the General Foods company, but we prefer not to use their preferred wording which would result in these being "Jell-O Brand Gelatin Dessert Popcorn Hearts." You may use a different brand if you wish, but then you may not call these Jell-O Popcorn Hearts unless you wish to risk a stay in Trademark Jail.

MARSHMALLOWS

What's a good old favorite like marshmallows doing in a book like this? Ah, but have you ever made your *own* marshmallows? Do you know anyone who has? See! Just because they've been around for years doesn't mean they can't be a bit unusual. Won't your friends be amazed when they learn that you did it all by yourself. All right, this is sort of like putting a "build your own washing machine" plan into a book of projects for the home craftsperson. Except that making marshmallows at home is easier, and one of the interesting aspects is that you can make them any size and shape you want. How about a marshmallow made in an interesting-shaped gelatin mold? How about a 12-pound marshmallow cube? How about a marshmallow rope six feet long?

Ingredients
1   envelope unflavored gelatin
⅓   cup cold water
⅔   cup light corn syrup
½   tsp. vanilla
½ cup + 3 or 4 tsp. sugar
4   tbsp. cornstarch

Preparation
• Soften the gelatin in cold water and dissolve in the top of a double boiler.
• Add ½ cup sugar, stirring until dissolved.
• Add the corn syrup and vanilla, and beat with an electric mixer at high speed until it looks like marshmallow. This may take as long as 15 minutes.
• For traditional-shaped marshmallows, sprinkle 2 tbsp. of sugar and 2 tbsp. of cornstarch on the bottom of a 9 x 9 x 2 pan.
• Pour in the marshmallow mixture and refrigerate one hour.
• Loosen from the pan and invert onto a board also sprinkled with 2 tbsp. sugar and 2 tbsp. cornstarch.
• Cut into marshmallow-sized pieces with a wet cold knife, and roll individual pieces in more sugar plus cornstarch.
• For other shapes, do what you will, as long as the finished product is coated with equal quantities of sugar and cornstarch.

NAVY BEAN AND PEANUT BUTTER COOKIES

We found, uh, located, well, that is, swiped this recipe from the pages of the Pontiac, Michigan *Press*, which we hereby thank. At first glance, it looks as if the beans are there just to fill things out, but this isn't quite the case: they change the texture as well. Once you've made the bean purée, you might add it to the other heavy baked goods (nut breads, muffins, and the like); it makes them better for you (more protein and all that). You can freeze the left over bean purée until you think of something else interesting to do with it (and/or decide to make another batch of these cookies).

Ingredients

2	cups sifted all-purpose flour		½	cup shortening
1	cup light brown sugar		1	cup peanut butter
1	cup granulated sugar		2	eggs
½	tsp. baking soda		1	tsp. vanilla
1½	tsp. baking powder		1	cup navy bean purée
½	tsp. salt		½	tsp. dry mustard

Preparation of navy bean purée

• Soak 2 cups washed navy beans in 4 cups hot water for 1 hour.
• Add 2 cups water, ½ tsp. dry mustard.
• Simmer 1½ hours.
• Push through a sieve while hot. Makes 4 cups

Preparation of the cookies

• Sift together the flour, both sugars, baking soda, and baking powder and salt.
• Cream the shortening and peanut butter.
• Beat the eggs and add, along with vanilla, to the peanut butter.
• Slowly add the flour mixture to the peanut butter mixture a little at a time, alternating it with the bean purée.
• Mix it all together and chill for 1 hour.
• Drop by spoonfuls on a greased cookie sheet,
• Bake 8 to 10 minutes at 375°.

Makes about 4 dozen cookies

PEACH LEATHER

ong ago, someone discovered that mashed peaches turn sort of leathery when exposed to the sun. Not quite leathery enough to make shoes from, but enough to give your teeth a good workout. The only problem is that you have to wait 3 or 4 months to find out how good this is, unless of course you have some left over from last year's batch.

Ingredients

    Fresh peaches
    Sugar

Preparation

- Peel and slice some soft peaches, and mash them with a fork.
- Pat them into a ¼–inch thick layer on a plate, and set out in the sun. (The peaches, that is; you may set with them if you wish.)
- The juices will thicken, and after a few hours or more, you will be able to lift the peach in one piece from the plate.
- Do so.
- Place in a stone crock on top of a layer of granulated sugar about ¼ inch thick.
- Spread another layer of sugar on top of the peach.
- Whenever the spirit moves and the peach tree is willing, make another layer of peaches, and add to the crock, always with layers of sugar in between. Finish up with sugar on top.
- In the fall, set the crock in a cool place, covered. The main enemy of fruit leather is moisture. Keep it dry, and it will last indefinitely. If you're worried about it, dig out a piece from time to time, cut off a chunk, and nibble. Call it research.
- Bring it out around Christmas time, or later if you wish. It will last indefinitely.

PEAR PIZZA

Nowhere in the Constitution or anywhere else is it written that pizza must be made with cheese, tomato sauce, and various meats and vegetables. We've discovered, or have been sent, a variety of recipes and suggestions for dessert pizza, and we especially like Judith Roth's approach, using apricot preserves instead of tomato sauce, and pears (or apples or peaches) instead of pepperoni. (Note: if you use apples or peaches, you probably should rename your creation accordingly.)

Ingredients for the crust
¾   cup sugar
8   tbsp. margarine
1   egg, beaten
½   cup flour
1   tsp. baking powder
¼   tsp. salt

Preparation of the crust
- Cream the sugar, margarine and egg together.
- Blend in flour, baking powder and salt.
- Pat the dough into a large flat circle on a 14-inch ungreased (you might want to use non-stick spray) pizza pan, or a cookie sheet.

Ingredients for the topping
½   jar apricot preserves
2   cups of pear slices or chunks, peeled or unpeeled as you wish
¼   cup sugar

Preparation of the pizza
- Spread the preserves on the raw cookie dough.
- Arrange the fruit on top of the preserves in a decorative manner, and sprinkle with sugar.
- Bake in a preheated 350º oven until the edges of the dough are golden brown (12-15 minutes).
- Cool, then cut into wedges and serve.

Serves 8 to 10

POTATO CHIP COOKIES

So you've heard of chocolate chip cookies, of course. Perhaps date and nut chip cookies. And now, thanks to Hope Wile in New York, the very person who came up with the name for this book, here come potato chip cookies. Don't fret about the salt. As long as you use unsalted butter, it will all come out just right. You might be especially daring and try a flavored potato chip, but not barbecued, please.

Ingredients
1   cup unsalted butter
½   cup sugar
1   tsp. vanilla
½   cup crushed potato chips
½   cup chopped pecans
2   cups sifted all-purpose flour

Preparation
• Preheat oven to 350º.
• Cream together butter, sugar, and vanilla.
• Add crushed potato chips and pecans.
• Stir in flour.
• Form into small balls, about 1 tbsp. of dough for each.
• Place them on an ungreased cookie sheet.
• Press the balls flat with the bottom of a glass that has been dipped in sugar. Before the first cookie-flattening, grease the bottom of the glass to make the sugar adhere. Our first tester, noticing that sugar did not adhere when she first dipped her glass, confessed that she just licked the glass bottom and it worked fine. We do not advocate this method, but we won't ask, either.
• Bake 16 to 18 minutes, until lightly browned. Cool on a rack.

Serves 42 people, if they eat one cookie each, or 1 person if he or she eats 42 cookies. Or somewhere in between.

PARSNIP CAKE

There are very few households where the words "parsnip" and "cake" would be used in the same sentence. One fortunate exception is the household of Dianne and Robert Drew iin New Zealand, who responded to our world-wide recipe search by sharing this creation. They write that this is a "wonderful cake, but everyone sneers when you tell them the ingredients in advance; often they won't even taste it. Obviously, the trick is to have them eat some, and then reveal all." The Drews recommend serving it with lemon cream frosting, and we quite agree.

Ingredients for cake
1   cup superfine sugar
1¼ cups vegetable oil
1   tsp. vanilla extract
3   eggs
½   cup crushed pineapple
4   cups grated parsnip
1⅓ cups flour
½   tsp. salt
1   tsp. baking soda
½   cup currants
2   tbsp. cinnamon

Ingredients for lemon cream cheese frosting
1   cup cream cheese
½   cup superfine sugar
5   ounces butter, melted
1   lemon (juice and rind)

Preparation of cake
• Grease a 9-inch springform pan
• Preheat oven to 350º.
• Whisk sugar, oil and vanilla.
• Add eggs one at a time beating well.
• Stir in pineapple.
• In a large bowl combine parsnip, flour, salt, baking soda, currants and cinnamon. Pour wet ingredients into this and combine.
• Bake for 1½ hours or when cake tester comes out clean.

Preparation of frosting
• Beat all ingredients together and frost cake once cold.

Serves 8

PINTO BEAN FUDGE

Long ago, when we ran a small candy store and factory (The Flying Bear, in Fort Bragg, California), we used to make a "mystery fudge" every month, with a modest prize for the first person who guessed the secret ingredient. We used cheddar cheese, we used tomato soup, but it never occured to us to use pinto beans, so we were delighted when Ruth Tisdale shared this recipe with us.

Ingredients

6   ounces unsweetened chocolate
6   tbsp. butter
1   cup cooked pinto beans, drained
      and mashed
¼ to ½ cup milk
1   tbsp. vanilla
2   pounds powdered sugar
      Optional raisins and/or nuts

Preparation

• Melt chocolate and butter.
• Add mashed pinto beans mixed with milk. Start with ¼ cup.
• Add 1 tbsp. vanilla.
• Stir until slightly thickened.
• Gradually work in the powdered sugar. If it gets too thick, add a bit more of the milk.
• Spread in buttered pan.
• Stir in raisins and/or nuts if you wish.
• Refrigerate.

Ingredients Quiz
Which of these three kinds of pintos should you use in this recipe? *(Answer at bottom)*

A.

B.

C.

Answer to Quiz
They will all work, but A. will make a tastier fudge.

POTATO CHOCOLATE CAKE

Yum yum. A chocolate-covered potato on a stick. No? Let's try again. How about mashed potatoes with chocolate chips? No? How about a potato-flavored candy bar? Oh, all right, in the quest for a tasty way to combine potatoes and chocolate, we defer to Susan Colledge, who provided us with this very satisfactory recipe for a potato chocolate cake (with lots of other nice ingredients as well).

Ingredients

⅔ cup butter, softened
2 cups sugar
4 eggs
1 cup hot instant mashed potato
2 squares unsweetened chocolate, melted
2 cups sifted all purpose flour
3½ tsp. baking powder
1 tsp. cinnamon
½ tsp. nutmeg
½ tsp. ground cloves
½ tsp. mace
½ cup milk
1 cup chopped nuts

Preparation

• Cream butter and sugar until light and fluffy.
• Add eggs, one at a time, beating thoroughly after each.
• Add mashed potato and chocolate and mix well.
• Sift dry ingredients together and add alternatively with milk, beating after each
   addition until smooth.
• Stir in nuts.
• Pour into greased and floured 9 x 13 x 2 pan.
• Bake at 350° 35 minutes or until done (when a toothpick, inserted int he middle,
   comes out clean.) Cool in pan, or turn out on cake rack to cool. Frost.

Serves 12

PUMPERNICKEL ICE CREAM WITH BRANDY

People have been making dark-bread-flavored ice cream for hundreds of years. But not very often, which is a pity, since it has a most unusual, mysterious, and altogether delightful sort of flavor. You can make ice cream out of whole wheat, Jewish rye (seedless, please) or pumpernickel. We prefer the pumpernickel (only in part because it's more fun to say), but they are all good.

Ingredients
3   egg yolks
1½   cups sugar
1   tsp. vanilla
4   cups heavy cream
¾   cup day-old pumpernickel bread
2   tbsp. brandy

Preparation
• Mix the egg yolks, sugar, and vanilla until very smooth.
• Heat the cream not quite to the boiling point, and add to the egg-sugar mixture.
• Crumble the bread and add.
• Beat thoroughly until smooth again.
• Heat again to just below the boiling point.
• Add brandy and stir.
• Let cool to room temperature.
• Pour into freezer trays and freeze until mushy.
• Beat once again and return to the freezer until frozen.

Serves 6-8

SEAWEED BLANCMANGE

Blancmange is a sort of Jell-O-ish puddingish type of dessert, normally flavored with vanilla. You may, if the ingredients are available and the heart is stout, make it with seaweed. In particular, you should make it with Irish Moss, also known as carrageen, which may be found on many European beaches as well as in the northeastern US and southeastern Canada. You may be more likely, however, to find it in health food stores and drug stores. In processed form, it's found in Chinese markets. where it's usuallly identified as agar-agar.

Ingredients
¾   cup seaweed
4   cups milk
    sugar
    salt
½   tsp. lemon extract or vanilla
    cream

Preparation
• Soak the seaweed in cold water for 5 minutes.
• Tie it up in a cheesecloth bag and cook, in the top of a double boiler* with milk and a dash of salt, for 30 minutes.
• Remove the bag full of seaweed, and discard it.
• Add lemon or vanilla to the pot, pour into bowls, and chill until firm.
• Serve with sugar and cream.

Serves 4

---

* Cookbooks always say it this way. Does anyone ever cook anything on the *bottom* of a double boiler besides water?

SELF-CRUSTING APPLE PIE

If a fudgy cake can make its own frosting as it cooks (see the very next page) is there any reason why an apple pie cannot make its own crust as *it* cooks? There is not. And so this one does. Or, at least, it *almost* does. This is not your ordinary flaky crust—more of a biscuity crust. And try as it will, it cannot make a complete crust that covers the whole pie, but it comes close, doing the entire bottom, sides, and some of the top. What more can you ask? (*Note:* you can substitute mincemeat for the apples if you wish.)

Ingredients
1   cup all purpose flour
1   tsp. baking powder
½   tsp. salt
1   tbsp. sugar
1   egg
⅔   cup shortening
¾   cup water
1   can (21-ounce) apple pie filling
1   tbsp. lemon juice
½   tsp. apple pie spice

Preparation
• Blend the flour, baking powder, salt, sugar, egg, shortening, and water together in a small mixer bowl.
• Beat at medium speed for 2 minutes.
• Pour into 9-inch pie pan.
• Mix pie filling, lemon juice, and spice together and pour into center of batter.
• Do not stir. Bake at 425° for 50 minutes.

Note: For purists among us, you *can* use fresh apples in this recipe. Combine 2½ cups peeled, sliced apples, with ⅓ cup sugar, 2 tablesoons of flour, and ½ tsp. apple pie spice. Dump that into the center of the batter and bake as above.

Serves 6

SELF-FROSTING UPSIDE-DOWN FUDGY CAKE

By some chemical-type magic we do not purport to understand, those parts of the ingredients of this cake which belong in the frosting separate themselves from those parts of the ingredients which belong in the cake, and by the time the darn thing is cooked, it has a regular frosting right where it should be—which is, of course, on the bottom, because it is also an upside-down cake.

Ingredients
½ cup + 2 tbsp. butter
1¼ cups all purpose flour
¾ cup sugar
2½ tsp. baking powder
⅔ cup milk
½ tsp. salt
2 ounces unsweetened chocolate, melted
2 eggs
½ cup pecan halves
¾ cup chocolate syrup
½ cup water

Preparation
• Melt 2 tbsp. butter into a 9-inch square pan and set aside.
• Mix the flour, sugar, baking powder, milk, salt, chocolate, and eggs together in a mixer bowl.
• Beat for 2 minutes at medium speed.
• Pour into square pan.
• Sprinkle pecans on top.
• Mix syrup and water together and spoon over the batter.
• Do not stir in.
• Bake at 350º for 40 minutes.
• Cool for 2 minutes.
• Invert onto serving plate.
• Serve with whipped cream or ice cream.

Serves about 8

189

SIX-MONTH BRANDIED FRUIT CROCK

More than three decades ago, our then-friend Mark Lawrence, semi-famous for producing his first and perhaps only film, a charming movie called *David and Lisa*, decided to make movie number 2, and acquired the rights to a wonderful little book called *Instant Gold*, by Frank O'Rourke. In the book, protagonist Trevisan Fundador creates an everlasting fruit crock, which may, in fact, have been the best (surely the tastiest) part of the book. Sadly, the movie never came to pass, but the everlasting fruit crock—at least our interpretation thereof—survives. Please note that it will take about six months to come into its own. One interesting strategy is to start it when the first pineapples bloom in spring, and plan to eat it at your Thanksgiving feast. Absolutely not for children and other non-drinkers.

Ingredients

1   pint Cherry Heering liqueur
1   pint brandy

At least five of the following:

1 quart strawberries	1 quart wild cherries
1 quart pineapple cubes	1 pint grapes
1 quart peeled sliced apricots	1 quart peeled sliced peaches
	1 pint blackberries
	1 quart raspberries
	Lots of sugar

Preparation

• Pour the liquor into a large stone crock with a tight-fitting lid.
• Add the fruit whenever you wish, as it comes into season or on special at the store.
• Each time you add fruit, add an equal quantity, by weight, of sugar. 1 pound of cherries, 1 pound of sugar, and so on.
• Keep the crock in the refrigerator, and give it a stir every couple of days.
• Nibbling may be permitted starting in month four, but it is best after six months.

SODA CRACKER TOFFEE

Toffee is traditionally made by heating up brown sugar and butter, and letting it harden on a cold slab. It is not known as a diet food. Understatement of the week. We bring you, now, Peggy Battles of Amarillo, Texas, whose method for making toffee consists of pouring the syrup onto soda crackers, of all things. The end result is delightfully toffee-like, but fully half of what you are eating is crackers, not butter and sugar. Still not diet food (especially with Ms. Battle's proposal to add a chocolate topping), but a wee bit better for you, perhaps. Why even think about it. Just don't eat the whole batch at one sitting, tempted though you may be.

Ingredients
1   cup sugar
½   pound butter (unsalted)
40   soda crackers
2½   cups chocolate chips (dark or milk, as you wish, even mint-flavored)

Preparation
• Line two 11 x 16 cookie sheets with aluminum foil.
• Cover entirely with soda crackers (one layer deep).
• In a saucepan, mix sugar and butter and bring to a rolling boil.
• Pour this over the crackers.
• Bake 12-15 minutes at 350° (until well browned).
• Immediately sprinkle the chocolate chips on top, and spread them around evenly.
• Put the whole shebang into the freezer.
• When the toffee hardens, you can break it into pieces if you wish.

STRING BEAN, SPAGHETTI AND CHOCOLATE PIE FLAMBÉ

Here is one of our favorites from the Recipe Game. It is incredibly chocolatey, rather chewy, and awfully good, if we do say so ourselves (and we do). No one will ever believe that one of the main ingredients is string beans. For some reason, string beans in these quantities tend to enhance the flavor of the chocolate. We made this with and without beans, and we thought it was actually better with.

Ingredients

1   box (13 ounce) chocolate frosting mix (or 2 cups of your favorite chocolate frosting)
1   box instant chocolate pudding
8   inch graham cracker pie crust
8   ounce can string beans
4   ounces spaghetti or macaroni
¼   cup crème de cacao or Vandermint liqueur

Preparation

• Mix up the chocolate frosting according to the directions on the box.
• Drain the string beans very well, dice them, and stir into the chocolate mix.
• Break the spaghetti into small pieces (about 1 inch) and boil until cooked but firm (*al dente*).
• Stir the spaghetti into the string bean-chocolate mixture.
• Stir in the chocolate pudding mix and 1 tbsp. liqueur.
• Mix well.
• Turn into the pie crust and refrigerate at least two hours.
• Just before serving, heat the remaining liqueur in a saucepan until it catches fire, pour over the pie, and serve while still flaming (you'll have to move fast).

> **THE RECIPE GAME**
> One player writes the names of five to seven ingredients on slips of paper, and puts them in a bowl or bag. The other player draws out three slips, and is required to create a recipe using those three ingredients in meaningful amounts. No fair putting a tiny crumb of anchovy in the chocolate apricot soufflé. When we played it, there was a satisfactory result at least half the time.

Serves 6 to 8

STRAWBERRY PRETZEL JELL-O

We've read that the trolley car was invented, almost at the same moment, by two people in different parts of the country, each one having no idea that the other was doing the same thing. Well the same phenomenon seems to have occurred in the matter of strawberry pretzel Jell-O salad. Sherri Morris write to us that a friend of hers made it "many moons ago" and gave her the recipe. And, at the same time, Marsha Shlaer shared with us her version, as adapted from a recipe she once found in the Augusta Chronicle. Maybe not as practical as the trolley car, but a lot more tasty.

Ingredients for the crust
2   cups pretzels, whirled to small bits in a food processor (or laboriously crushed with a rock—your choice)
3   tbsp. sugar
1   cup butter, melted

Preparation of crust
• Combine the ingredients and put in a ungreased 9 x 13 baking pan.
• Bake for 10 minutes at 350°.
• Allow to cool completely.

Ingredients for middle layer
1   bar of cream cheese, (At room temperature it's easiest to mix.)
1   cup sugar
1   8-ounce container of cool whip

Ingredients for top layer
2   10 ounce packages of sweetened frozen strawberries
1   6 ounce package of strawberry Jell-O (or 2 - 3oz packages)
2   cups hot water

Preparation
• Combine middle-layer ingredients with a mixer until smooth.
• Spread evenly onto crust
• Combine Jell-O and hot water.
• When Jell-O is dissolved add the frozen strawberries.
• Let mixture sit in the refrigerator for 20-25 minutes
• Pour the Jell-O-strawberry mixture on the cream cheese.
• Chill in refrigerator overnight,

TOMATO SOUP CAKE

Some of us are old enough to remember when carrot cake really seemed unusual. This cookbook invites a number of other vegetables to express themselves in like manner. Here is a contribution sent to us by Karen Alexander of Winnipeg, Manitoba to join the ever-growing list. In some sort of mystical alchemy, the tomato soup, combined with the other ingredients, ends up tasting spicy, rich, and delicious. We don't think the cake especially needs a frosting, but if *you* do, any sort of simple vanilla or orange or spice frosting will do fine. Or top it with applesauce. (*Note:* the smells in the house while this is cooking will be splendid.)

Ingredients

½   cup butter
1   cup brown sugar
1   egg
1   tsp. nutmeg
1   tsp. cinnamon
½   tsp. cloves
½   tsp. salt
1   cup raisins
1   10-ounce can tomato soup
1   tsp. baking soda

Preparation

• In a bowl, mix the first eight ingredients.
• Empty the soup can into this mixture.
• Stir the baking soda into the residue of soup in the nearly-empty soup can, and
    don't fret if it goes a bit fizzy.
• Add to mixture in the bowl. Stir in flour.
• Bake in 9 x 13 pan at 350° for 40 to 45 minutes.
• When cool, top with frosting if you wish,
    not, please, with croutons.

Serves 8-10

VELVEETA™ PEPPERMINT FUDGE AND SIMPLE VELVEETA™ FUDGE

Elsewhere in this volume, we introduce the excellent chocolate cheese that comes from Michigan State University. But if you have not yet placed your order with the Dairy Store in East Lansing, yet crave the cheese and chocolate combo experience, here are two ways to achieve that result: an extremely simple one, and, thanks to Alice Tillerson, a somewhat more complex one with the added bonus of crunchy peppermint bits.

SIMPLE VELVEETA FUDGE

Ingredients
1	pound margarine or butter		4	pounds powdered sugar
1	pound Velveeta cheese		2	cups chopped nuts (optional)
1	cup cocoa		2	tsp. vanilla extract

Preparation
• Melt butter/margarine and cheese together over low heat, stirring constantly.
• Mix in remaining ingredients.
• Spread in greased 9 x 13 inch pan and cool. Cut in squares and refrigerate.
(*Note:* Works fine at half the above quantities)

LESS-SIMPLE VELVEETA PEPPERMINT FUDGE

Ingredients
12	ounces Velveeta		2	tbsp. light corn syrup
1	cup (2 sticks) butter or margarine		1	tsp. vanilla extract
6	squares Bakers unsweetened baking chocolate		2	pounds powdered sugar, sifted
			½	cup crushed peppermint candies

Preparation
• Cut cheese into small pieces.
• Add cheese to a 3-quart saucepan along with butter, chocolate and corn syrup.
• Cook on medium-low heat until smooth, stirring occasionally.
• Pour into a large bowl, and gradually add sugar, beating with an electric mixer (medium speed) until well blended.
• Stir in vanilla and peppermint.
• Pour into greased 9x13 pan.
• Smooth with a spatula.
• Refrigerate for at least two hours, then cut into squares (or any other shape you darn well please).

WACKIE CAKE FROM ST. JOHN THE EVANGELIST

The Parish hall over at St. John the Evangelist Church in Moriches, New York, must be a rather jolly place, at least when Wendy Toto is around. We deduce this from her recipe, as published in 1978 their *One Day at a Time Cookbook,* kindly shared with us by Judith Roth. The use of vinegar is a little "wackie," and the "three hole" method of preparation is a bit "wackie" as well, but the end result is a simple, basic, tasty cake.

Ingredients

1½	cups flour		dash of salt
1	cup sugar	5	tbsp. oil
3	tbsp. cocoa	1	tbsp. vinegar
1	tsp. baking soda	1	tsp. vanilla
1	tsp. baking powder	1	cup warm water

Preparation

• Sift the 6 dry ingredients together into an 8 or 9 inch square pan.
• Make three holes in this mixture.
• In the first, put the oil.
• In the second, put the vinegar.
• In the third, put the vanilla. Pour the water over it all, and mix well with a fork.
• Bake in a preheated 350° oven for 30 minutes.

Serves 9 (3" squares)

WAFFLE IRON BROWNIES

This intriguing recipe has come to us fourth-hand, and we're still not sure whose invention it is. In the interest of historical cuisinology, we here with report that Judith Roth sent it to us, from a book in which Constance Hay writes it up, and says it was given to her by her friend Laura Schrader, and for all we know, Laura found it tacked to a bulletin board at Buckingham Palace. In any event, it fits in well with our sub-theme of using household appliances in unexpected ways

Ingredients

½   cup butter or margarine
¼   cup unsweetened cocoa powder
¾   cup granulated sugar
2   eggs, well beaten
1   tbsp. water
1¼ cups all-purpose flour
¼   tsp. salt
⅔   cup chopped walnuts (optional)
    confectioners sugar (optional)

Preparation

• Preheat the waffle iron at a medium setting.
• Melt butter or margarine in a saucepan over low heat.
• Remove from heat.
• Using a wooden spoon, blend in the cocoa powder, then the sugar, eggs and water.
• Add flour and salt and beat well.
• Add the optional nuts (ifyou are making these for John, please don't).
• If your waffle iron has four sections (most do), drop one well-rounded teaspoon of batter onto each quarter.
• Close the lid and cook for about 1½ minutes.
• Test them by raising the lid a wee bit; they should not stick to the top. If they need detaching, use a wooden skewer or toothpick.
• Cool on a rack.
• Sprinkle with optional sugar.

Makes about 30 brownies

BEER FLOAT

Float: a scoop of tasty frozen stuff in a big glass of tasty liquid stuff. The possibilities are endless. Indeed some are classic: vanilla ice cream in a glass of root beer (root beer float), chocolate ice cream in a glass of cream soda, cherry ice cream in a cherry cola. And, in this less common variation, a big scoop of ice cream (preferably vanilla) in a cold glass of beer (preferably light). The idea was sent to us aneonymously (thank you anyway) by someone who suggests that "it sort of tastes like any ice cream drink, but with a hops undertaste."

Ingredients
1   large glass of beer (preferably light)
1   large scoop of ice cream (preferably vanilla)

Preparation
• Add the second item to the first.

BLAZING SCOTCH WATERFALL

Rest assured—you will not need to waste three gallons of scotch practicing this so you can put on an amazing performance for your guests. It's remarkably easy. What happens is that you end up pouring a flaming mixture back and forth from one container to another, preferably in a darkened room. The effect is that of a continuous streak of blue fire dancing about your front. Please be careful not to set your necktie or beard on fire.

Ingredients
    scotch
    water
    honey
    match

Preparation
- You'll need two heatproof mugs.
- Fill one just under half full of very hot water with a tablespoon of honey stirred in.
- Fill the other just under half full of very hot scotch.

Note: You can microwave each mug, separately, for about 45 seconds.

- Set fire to the scotch; pour it very quickly into the mug with the water; pour the mixture back into the first mug; and so on, until the two are thoroughly mixed, and the fire has gone out.

CHILLED SPAM AND ANCHOVY SHAKE

Long ago, we were part-owners of a small ice cream factory in Fort Bragg, California. While we were busily making quite lovely chocolates, vanillas, and the like, the idea arose for non-sweet food-flavored ice creams. If cold soups such as gazpacho and vichysoisses work, we reasoned, why not roast beef ice cream (with horseradish sauce), corned beef ice cream (with cabbage sauce), and the like. However, we were never able to persuade our partners to give it a try. The very prospect of expunging all of the anchovies (for instance) from our one and only freezing machine, was daunting. Well, in this recipe, that same direction of food content and temperature is addressed, without the need for risking a large and expensive piece of equipment.

Ingredients
1   can of Spam
1   tin of anchovies
2   12oz cans of beer
4   oz tomato juice
1   tsp. Dijon mustard
½   cup chopped up parsley
¼   cup chopped scallions
     dash of Tabasco
     salt (if you wish), pepper to taste

Preparation
• Put it in blender and blend until smooth.
• Serve chilled with celery stick.

Serves 3 or 4

USE AT YOUR OWN RISK.
If you do try this, please write a review and send it to the publisher. Writers of the five best reviews received— good, bad, or otherwise— will get one free cookbook published by SLG Books. Send your review (3 to 300 words) by November 5, 2003 to
SLG Books
P. O. Box 9465
Berkeley, CA 94709
Decision of the judge is final.

FLAMING ENGLISH PUNCH

This is not descriptive of the knockout blow delivered by Dauntless Darryl Brock in his famous battle for the Lightweight Championship of Gloucestershire. It is, rather, a most delicious and quite spectacular beverage. By soaking the sugar in the rum, and then setting the two afire, the taste changes in an interesting way, with just a hint of caramel from the burned sugar. Any kind of red wine will do, but we think Bordeaux is best.

Ingredients

3   cups strong tea
6   cups red wine
1   pound granulated sugar
1   lemon
1   orange
1   fifth rum

Preparation

• Mix the wine and tea together.
• Add the juice from the lemon and orange.
• Heat well, and pour into a heat-resistant punch bowl.
• Soak the sugar in the rum, and heat both in a saucepan.
• Ignite, let burn as long as it will, and stir well into the punch.

Makes about 3 quarts

QUEEN ANNE'S SECRET TEA WITH WINE AND EGG YOLKS

Queen Anne of England was, by all accounts, not a happy monarch. Although pregnant seventeen times, none of her children survived to adulthood, and when she died before her fiftieth birthday, she had no heirs, and there went the Stuart line. After her death, it was discovered that she kept secret diaries, which included some recipes. We assume she kept this recipe secret because she thought it was so remarkably good, it shouldn't be given to the masses, and not because she didn't want her subjects to know she was on the sauce. No matter. Great stuff.

Ingredients

4   eggs
2   cups white wine
4   cups tea
¼   cup sugar

Preparation

• Beat the egg yolks until they thicken.
• Add everything else slowly, and cook over medium heat until thickened slightly.
• Serve in hot mugs.
• Sprinkle nutmeg on top if you wish.

Serves 8 or more.

VEGEMITE MILKSHAKE

(see page 12)

In Marina's family's Russian tradition, one drinks hot tea by holding a sugar cube in the front teeth, and then pouring the tea into the mouth around the cube. In a bizarre way, this Australian approach to milkshakes achieves the same thing. An incredibly hot piece of pepper is held in the front of the mouth, and the milkshake is poured in around it. The shake itself is made from Vegemite, which some have called the Australian National Dish: an immensely popular form of yeast extract. But yeast extract is not that rare a creature, and can be found in health food stores, either in bulk or under various brand names, including Marmite. This recipe comes from an Australian website called "Greggles Place."

Ingredients

Vegemite (or other concentrated yeast extract goop, such as the British Marmite)

2 tbsp. chocolate milk powder (in Australia, it's Milo)
2 eggs
4 ounces low-fat milk
2 beef or chicken bouillon cubes
Large scoop of vanilla ice cream
1 very hot chili pepper
dash of nutmeg

Preparation

• Put the chocolate powder at the bottom of a large glass.
• Lightly spread the Vegemite over the powder, to 'seal in' the chocolate flavor.
• Beat the eggs and pour them on top of the Vegemite layer.
• Add the milk and bouillon to the glass.*
• Using an ice cream scoop, scoop out a big scoop of ice cream. While it is still in the scoop, cover generously with Vegemite, so that it is completely black.
• Carefully drop the Vegemite-covered ice cream ball into the glass from a height of 13 inches. (Mr. Greggles reports that at a lower height, the ice cream will sink; at a higher height, it may fracture the glass.)
• Sprinkle with nutmeg.
• Take a small piece of the chili pepper and chew it quickly, and then, even more quickly, take a swig or two of your shake.

---

* Greggles says nothing whatever about dissolving the bouillon or stirring it in. What do you think?

HOW THIS BOOK GOT ITS TITLE AND ITS COVER

We first had the idea for this book so many years ago that even our language was different. We were calling it, for heaven's sake, *The Kook Book*. When the project was resurrected, under the fine auspices of SLG Books, it was clear that a new name was needed, since no one had intentionally used the word "kook" or "kookie" since 1974.

The Title

We put the word out to all friends and family members, and to a bunch of internet news groups, encouraging creativity by offering a $500 prize to the person who came up with the final title. Several hundred title suggestions came floating in, including many we liked. After much thought and discussion, we narrowed it down to these ten finalists, listed here alphabetically*

Cooking Outside the Box (Joanna Enderlin)
Flabbergastronomy (John Bear)
Not Your Mother's Cookbook (Hope Wile)
Now That's Interesting (Phyllis Yee)
Off the Wall and Onto Your Plate (Gus Sainz)
Quirky Cuisine (Bill Highsmith)
*Recipes that call for **what***? (Tami Ellinport)
Strange Breadfellows (Ellen Crowley)
The Adventuresome Cook (Nicole Ballard)
The Unusual, Please (Laura McClurg)

We really leaned toward *Strange Breadfellows,* but the distributor, whose sales people have a lot to say about such matters, felt it was a bit obscure, and the book was not about bread anyway. And so we went with our other favorite, adding "*Unusual recipes for the Adventuresome Cook*" as the subtitle—except that the distributor felt that "adventurous" was a better word. So be it. The $500 prize was shared by Hope Wile (the lion's share) and Nicole Ballard (the lamb's share), and then we moved on to the complex (as it turned out) matter of cover design.

The Cover

We liked the idea of illustrating "not your mother" with a nice old-fashioned mother, in the red circle with diagonal that most people means "Not" or "Don't." Like this:

No way. The all-important sales and marketing people said that you can't put a big red slash mark right through

---

* And thanks, too, to all the other title-suggesters: Betty Arehart, Maria Elena Monaco, Bill Huffman, Tracy Gies, Tom Hogan, Neil Hynd, Quinn Tyler Jackson, "Gerstl," and Dave Zeryck.

your mother; that neither the bookstore buyers nor the bookbuying public would stand for this.

All right, cancel the red line through the sweet old lady. But how about the same approach, using a younger mother, preferably one from the 1940s or 1950s who might be seen as a bit less adventurous than cooks today. We tried, but the young mother was shot down by the marketing people as well.

And so the next step—and the eventual solution— lay in the direction of having our original older mother doing something a bit outrageous in the kitchen. No, not tap dancing to the Sex Pistols or roller blading along the counter top. But taking something unusual, perhaps something from this very book, from her nice old-fashioned oven.

We believed we had the perfect dish: the visually stunning and very tasty Stargazy Pie, as described on page 91, with the six little sardines poking their heads through the crust to see the stars. Through the miracle of computer wizardry, we replaced the roast turkey in the original drawing with a stargazy pie, and we loved the result.

Alas, once again (but for the last time!), the sales people's thumbs turned downward. No way, they said. No one wants to buy a book that hints they are going to have to eat little fish heads.

But they liked the con-cept. The woman is taking something interesting and unusual out of the oven. Hot dogs? How about hot dogs. We rather liked the recipe for Crown Roast of Hotdog, as presented on page 51. With the power of PhotoShop, we electronically yanked the Stargazy Pie from her hands, and replaced it with the Crown Roast you see on the front of this very book (unless, of course, a last-minute change brought about something entirely different).*

Ah, the joys of writing, publishing, and bookselling in this modern age. As John's grandmother (who didn't look anything like this lady) used to say, "Go figure."

---

* And so it did! At the last possible moment, in marched the wonderful Stanley Mouse, and the result is what you now see on the cover.

THANKS

We have four categories of people to thank for their help in bring this book into existence. Without further ado, we'd better get cracking.

Recipe contributors

The recipes in this book came from many places, ranging from our own minds to semi-anonymous (we have E-mail addresses but no names) internet sources. Especially fertile sources were Nicole Ballard, and Judith Roth and her home economics class at Islip High School in Islip, New York, some of whom are shown below, and their names would be in gold if we could afford gold ink. In addition to their contributions, they also tested a bunch of the recipes, so we are doubly grateful. Go Buccaneers!

We have included recipes sent to us by all of the following people, whom we thank wih their name up in lights (so to speak), and an autographed copy of this very book: Harriet Abell, Sindy Albritton, Karen Alexander, Bernice Arnett , Peggy Battles, Jim Campbell, Dr. Vicky Campagna, "Cajun Lou," Susan Colledge, Ellen Crowley, "David and Penny," Robert & Dianne Drew, Sabrina Doster, Nelson H. Finkelman, S. I. Hayakawa, BillLaCroix, Paul Gasparo, "Jennifer," "Marlee," Laura McClurg, Marie Elena Monaco, Don M. McDonald, Sherri Morris, "Nora," Porfirio Rubinstein, "Shereen," Martha Shlaer, Christine Smith, Eddie Thompson, Alice Tillerson, Ruth Tisdale, Wendy Toto, Michael and Melissa Velik, Hope Wile, and Brenda Voss.

Recipe testers

With the exception of the half-dozen-or-so "Extreme Cuisine" recipes (see page 12 for an explanation), all of the recipes in the book were tested and, when necessary, modified. The great majority of the testing was done by our hard-working, conscientious, and talented twin daughters, who worked so hard at this project, over many months, they deserve at least a slightly larger typeface:

Miss Roth's Home Ec Class at Islip High School, Islip, New York

From left to right: Jennifer Bonilla, Andrew Parsons, Erin Shaffer, Lindsay Brown, Melissa Perry, Patty Whitney, Nancy Prior, teacher Judith Roth, Juan Alvarez, Anthony Arellano, Evan Brownell, Rob Thomas, and Jeff Signorelli. Not pictured (because we didn't get photos), but thanks as well, to Ashley Dansby, Nyleen Delgado, Amy Espinal, Daniel Gangi, Candy Gates, Melissa Hainey, Kristen Lane, Crystal Lindsey, Elyse Lyons, Nicole Massaro, Crystal Ortiz, Matthew Rivera, Megan Ryerson, Philip Smith, Kristin Squire, William Veryzer, and Alisha Wesley.

THANK YOU, SUSANNAH LUJAN-BEAR AND TANYA ZERYCK!

In addition to Ms. Roth's class, other recipes were tested by Nicole Ballard, Carolyn Bennett, Ira Trombley and William Highsmith. Thank you one and all.

Publishers and Distributors

This is our thirty-somethingth book, but our first for SLG Books and what a pleasure it has been, working with their professional staff, especially publisher Roger Williams and designer/editor Yuk Wah Lee.

Food and Cooking Editors

The sale of books like this depend a good deal on publicity, and getting publicity depends a good deal on the kindness of our nation's food and cooking editors. When his project was but a gleam in our eyes, we wrote to 156 US and Canadian food editors, telling then what we were up to, and asking for their help in finding unusual recipes. Some responded with splendid articles, some ignored us, and some were in between. We'd like to thank them all for their time, and the good they do for the cookbook publishing industry. [This is, of course, also a shameless effort to curry favor by putting their names up in (very small) lights.] Thanks to: Vickie Ashvill, April Austin, Elaine Ayala, Letitia Baldwin, Cathy Barber, Lee Barnes, Cate Barron, Michael Bauer, Jaye Beeler, Richard Bennett, Patty Beutler, Rosemary Black, David Bock, Ted Brockish, Oby Brown, Frank Brown, Gary Brown, Becky Buckingham, Beverly Bundy, Frieda Bush, Betsey Buzior, Steve Cagle, Terry Campbell, Debra Carr-Elsing, Philip Case, Sandy Thorn Clark, Joan Nam Coong, Joe Crea, Kitty Crider, Dale Curry, Claire Cusick, Jim Dagar, Molly Davis, Lee Dean, Gary Demuth, Allesandra Djurklov, Jane Dornbusch, Sharon Dowell, Tara Duggan, Mike Dunn, Louise G. Durman, Sara Ervanian, Judy Evans, Ruth Fantasia, Ellie Ferriter, Linda Fjeldsted, Melinda Forbes, Sarah Fortschner, Beth Gallaspy, Christine Arpe Gang, Tom Gearhart, Tim Ghiani, Linda Gillia, Lean Gilman, Linda Giuca, Kari Granville, Judy Grigoraci, Sarah Hale, Kendall Hamersly, Ann Heller, Laura Hengstier, Elizabeth Holland, Barbara Houle, Susan Houston, Kathie Jenkins, Scott Johnson, Jennifer Johnson, Keith Jones, Carolyn Jung, Sandy Kallio, John Katsilometes, Janet Keeler, Andy Kehe, Louise Kennedy, Mark Kennedy, John Kessler, Ron Krueger, Madelyn Lamb, Diane Lamorte, Rusty Lang, Lanny Larson, Donna Lee, Lori Linenberge, Debbie Lord, Julie Mack, Louis Mahoney, Tim Makinen, Kim Marcum, Jane P. Marshall, Chuck Martin, Suzanne Martinson, Kim McAuliffe, Steve McKinstry, Jeanne McManus, Murray McMillan, Carol McQuaid, Marty Meitus, Marty Meitus, Ronda Miskelley, T. C. Mitchell, Mara Mornell, Debby Morse, Elizabeth Munding, Jill Nevels-Haun, Paul Nussbaum, Kathy O'Gorman, Jo Ellen O'Hara, Jennifer O'Neil, Janice Okun, Wanda Owings, Christa Palmer, Jane Palmer, Rosemary Parrillo, Russ Parsons, Cynthia Pasquale, Valerie Phillips, Steve Plesa, Grant Podelco, Susan Puckett, Kathi Purvis, William Rice, Jackie Rice, Olivia Ridgell, Alicia Roberts, Ken Rogers, Chris Rubich, Ann Rutter, Vivian Salazar, Richard Sandell, Peggy Santoro, Betty Shimabukuro, Phyllis Sigal, Jill Silva, Christy Slewinski, Richard Slusser, Jane Snow, Lisa Sodders, Diane Stoneback, Polly Summar, Jim Swenson, Jeff Tiedeman, T. R. Titchko, Cleve Twitchell, Terri Vanech, Charlyne Varkonyi, Janet Vlieg, Sally Vornhagen, Judy Walker, Sarah Wallace, Cookie Walter, Irene Wassell, Patricia Watts, Suzanne White, Kristen Wilkison, Roger Williams, Connie Wirta, and Catherine Zaiser.